Living and Working with Bereavement

Guide for Widowed Men and Women

Elsie Palmer
Jill Watt

Detselig Enterprises Limited
Calgary, Alberta

© 1987 by
Elsie Palmer
Jill Watt

Canadian Cataloguing in Publication Data

Palmer, Elsie.
   Living and working with bereavement

   ISBN 0-920490-69-7

   1. Bereavement – Psychological aspects. 2.
   Grief. I. Watt, Jill, 1931- . II. Title.
   BF575.G7P3 1987   155.9'37   C87-091243-7

Detselig Enterprises Ltd.
P.O. Box G 399
Calgary, Alberta T3A 2G3

Printed in Canada   SAN-115-0324   ISBN 0-920490-69-7

Table of Contents

Acknowledgements

We wish to thank Vancouver freelance editor Beth Tetzel for her encouragement, suggestions and support. And we thank the widowed interviewees for the time they gave us and for their important contribution to *Living and Working with Bereavement*. (Names and some facts were altered to protect the identities of those interviewed.)

E.P. & J.W.

Detselig Enterprises Ltd. appreciates the financial assistance for its 1987 publishing program from

Alberta Foundation for the Literary Arts
Canada Council
Department of Communications
Alberta Culture

Part One

*The Grief Process
and Your Feelings*

1
The Process of Grief

Grief is the natural reaction to the loss of someone of importance in your life. All through your life you have faced separation, change, loss and grief in varying degrees.

But the feelings following the death of a spouse are overwhelming. Physical responses are disturbing and difficult to understand. Adjustment takes time, and you will seem to take two steps forward, then one back, before finally reaching the point where you can feel confident about the future.

Grief begins with a period of shock. During this time you won't feel the full impact of your loss; you will feel stunned and out of touch with reality. This numbness can last for a few days, weeks or even longer.

Once the numbness starts to wear off, the most painful part of the process begins. The feelings of anguish, desolation and despair are difficult to express in words.

Now, you begin to have a wide range of emotions. Along with sadness, depression, loneliness, anxiety, panic and fear, there is often guilt and nearly always anger.

You may find it hard to understand why you have angry feelings towards your spouse. You are naturally distressed at having to be without him or her for the rest of your life. You actually feel abandoned. You may direct your resentment towards others, such as doctors, God, a minister or relatives.

Guilt is another usual emotion. You believe that somehow you should have known better than to say and do some things that now seem unkind and inappropriate as you review your relationship with your mate. You may have the persistent feeling that your spouse would still be alive if a different treatment had been tried or the doctor had been called sooner. All these "if onlys" are very common feelings, and need to be talked about. It will help you to believe that you did what you thought was appropriate at the time, and as you review the past, you will gradually begin to think rationally.

Anxiety and panic can keep you feeling very unsettled. Your sense of security has gone and you are left wondering whether you can survive without your partner, handling all the details of daily living that your spouse took care of, and making decisions alone that you used to make together.

You also regret that you and your spouse didn't get the chance to do all the things you planned, that his or her life ended so soon.

Sadness, loneliness and depression are familiar to a bereaved person. Even after the intensity of your grief subsides somewhat, loneliness may persist. It can be lessened considerably by involvement with friends and interesting activities. This usually means making new friends, as you will probably have less contact with the social network you were part of when you were married.

Besides the emotional aspects of grief, you will have physical reactions such as frequent episodes of crying and sobbing, often uncontrollable.

Another disturbance may be changes in your sleeping pattern – having difficulty getting to sleep, waking up very early or sleeping more than usual.

Your appetite may decrease. Many grievers lose weight because they lose interest in preparing meals for themselves. Overeating may be a problem to those who use food as a source of comfort.

Restlessness is common. You find it difficult to settle down to a task. You feel the urge to get out of the house and then, almost as soon as you are out, you want to go home again.

You may also find you can't concentrate for more than short periods. At work, you may forget tasks that are part of your routine. You tend to be preoccupied with your grief, so more effort is required to perform at an acceptable level.

Your employer will probably expect you to return to work soon after the death, usually within a week. Many people find that getting back into their regular work routine gives them a sense of security. You will have to set your grief aside for these hours at work, but it is important to allow yourself time to "let go" when you get home. You will adjust more successfully if you allow expression of your grief.

It makes sense to continue your volunteer work to give your life some continuity, providing the work is satisfying and not too strenuous. If you find it burdensome in effort or in time, ask to be relieved of your duties for a while. You can decide later whether or not you want to resume.

It is not usually a good idea to take on new activities. The fewer big changes made while you are mourning, the better. However, once your grief subsides, you will benefit greatly by finding a new interest, volunteer work or employment.

In Chapter 2 we talk in greater detail about coping with the emotional and physical impact of your loss.

Anticipatory grief

Anticipatory grief is the loss you feel before your spouse dies, when you know ahead of time that there will be no recovery. Some widows have told us they started grieving when the doctor said the husband's illness was terminal. They felt the shock, then went through the next phase and finally faced the reality of the approaching loss, beginning to adjust before the husband died.

Anticipatory grieving does not mean that you do not miss your spouse's physical presence when he or she dies. Even if you had adjusted to being at home without him or her because your spouse was hospitalized for an extended period, your time would most likely have been taken up by hospital visits.

Some friends and associates may be critical of your "quick" recovery. They do not understand how much grieving you have done before your spouse died.

Letting go of the past

The emotions of sadness, loneliness, depression, fear, anger, guilt and disappointment come and go during the grief process.

After the initial period of strong emotions, turmoil and disorganization, you will begin to take an interest in your own plans for what you can do now to give your life meaning.

Following the pain of grief comes the time when you accept your loss, let go of your spouse and put the past into perspective so that you have energy to give to your own life. Reaching the point of accepting your loss will take some time, but doing your "grief work" will help.

You will still remember your life together – the good times, the funny times, and the tender moments. The feelings of loss will return on occasion, retriggered by some incident. You are not going back to the beginning of your grief to endure it again. You have not really backtracked. This is merely the way the mind works. Certain incidents remind us of feelings we have had before.

It takes time, tears, remembering and talking to adjust successfully.

Grief work

Doing your "grief work" means expressing your feelings and participating actively in your adjustment. Grief work consists of:

– Crying when you need to.

– Expressing your anger rather than holding it in. You can scream or yell in the shower, punch pillows, walk fast, scrub floors, hammer nails, chop wood, run, play a game of racquetball or change the furniture around – something you have to give your whole attention to for a while.

– Talking about your loss with someone who is willing to listen. This does not mean talking to everybody about how you feel; some people won't want to listen. You'll soon know who they are.

– Reviewing the part of your life you spent with your spouse. Look back at your relationship from the time you met. Get out your picture albums and reconstruct the past. If you find this too painful right now, do it a little later.

– Disposing of your spouse's clothes and personal effects except, of course, items you want to keep. Ask someone to be with you while you do this.

– Thinking about your spouse as a person with imperfections as well as good qualities, so that you remember the real person and not the idealized version you may have envisioned since he or she died. It might help to make a list of the things you liked and loved about your spouse as well as those that bothered you.

When you have completed your grief work to the point of letting go, say "good-bye" to your spouse. You may want to look at a picture while doing this. Keep telling yourself he or she is dead until you actually believe it. You may reach this point in the first few months of bereavement or not until long after the first anniversary of the death.

Building a new life

The final part of adjustment is reinvestment – transferring your love and energy to other things and relationships. This could be an entirely new interest or the renewal of an activity that gave you satisfaction earlier in your life. It is a new beginning and the building of a new life.

Myths

There are several persistent myths surrounding grief.

The length of the grieving period is one of the most common myths. It upsets us every time we read that someone "should" be over their grief by the end of six months, a year, or a year and a half, and that if they are still grieving after that time, they need psychiatric help. While the acute part of the grief process may be over by that time, the length of the grieving period can vary greatly, depending on how soon you realize that your partner is really dead, the kind of life you had before the death, and so on. The time it takes to adjust is such an individual matter that we would not attempt to guess how long you would take. We will discuss later some of the factors that may impede adjustment, and ways to avoid getting "stuck" in the grief process.

Another myth is that people never get over their grief or adjust to the loss. It is true that you are not the same after suffering such a traumatic loss, but you can function. You can continue with your life and you can feel good again. You will learn to cope. You will probably even become a much more understanding person with a greater appreciation of life than before.

Factors which prolong grief

There are personal circumstances and characteristics which can prolong your grief process. Some of the most important are:

1. Difficulty in talking about your feelings.

If you have always found it hard to talk about your feelings, it won't be easy to express your grief openly. However, putting your feelings into words and allowing a trusted person to share your sorrow is a step towards adjustment. If you find it impossible to share your feelings with others, at least let your feelings surface when you are alone.

2. Several losses occurring close together.

It is natural that the death within a year or two of more than one person who has been important to you – a spouse and a parent, for example – should cause extra stress. So many life changes at once will seem like too much to bear. You probably feel you have been singled out by fate, God or some unknown force to suffer more than most. This does not mean you will not make progress and adjust in time, but it usually takes longer and you may want extra emotional support. Talk with a trusted friend. Go to a bereavement self-help group. Arrange for professional grief counselling.

3. Earlier grief which has not been resolved.

If, sometime before your husband or wife died, another family member or close friend died, you may notice that you begin to feel that loss again, which adds to your present grief.

For instance, one couple whose son died in a motorcycle accident could never talk about his death. After the death of the husband years later, the widow realized that she had never allowed herself to grieve for her son. With help from a grief counsellor and a self-help bereavement group, she learned about the grief process and some ways to do her grief work.

4. Chronic health problems.

If you had a health disorder before your spouse died and it continues to cause you distress, be sure to get good medical care as well as grief counselling.

5. Violent death (e.g., vehicle accident, homicide).

If your spouse died violently, your grief may be particularly intense. The period of shock will be longer, and your anger and bitterness will naturally be very strong. It is a nightmarish experience. If you were there and saw what happened, you will carry the picture in your mind and go over the scene again and again. The police will be involved and you will have to repeat what you saw and heard many times.

No one should face a situation as difficult as this without special help. You will need lawyers, civic employees and financial experts as well as your family and friends. You may want to consult a grief counsellor to help you deal with the strong emotions you will feel while the investigation goes on and on.

Widows and widowers often feel they can't "let go" of the past and begin to adjust until the court case has been settled. They feel they are being held in limbo. However bleak your life may look at present, you can make a successful adjustment. The inquiries and hearings will come to an end eventually, and you can get your life back in balance.

6. Death when you also are injured.

Accidental death is usually sudden and sometimes violent. Having a healthy spouse's life cut short by a car accident, industrial disaster, fire or riot is devastating. If you also were injured and hospitalized, you will be coping with extra pain. You will need to heal physically in addition to grieving the loss of your spouse.

7. Death by suicide.

As in the case of a violent death, grief after a suicide will likely be more complex and last longer than that following death from "natural causes."

If your spouse made several suicide attempts before actually taking her life, you may have already realized that, despite all efforts to dissuade your spouse, she was determined to die. Although many widowed people feel guilty, it is not realistic to think that you could have prevented it. It is common to have some sense of relief from worrying and from the helplessness of being unable to motivate your husband or wife to want to live.

If you were not aware of any prior warning and your spouse's suicide came as a sudden, shattering blow, there is often a feeling of guilt and an erroneous belief that some action on your part could have prevented it.

Your children may also blame themselves for saying or doing something which disappointed their father and caused him to kill himself.

No one causes someone else to take his own life. Like all of us, you will sometimes have been impatient with your husband or wife and responded with a lack of understanding. This does not make you responsible for the death. People commit suicide for so many reasons that the literature on the subject is quite extensive (see suggested reading section).

Talk about your feelings of guilt and bitterness to diminish and eventually eliminate any damaging effects they might have on your physical and emotional health. See that your children have an opportunity to express their feelings also. Talking with someone besides your family – for example, a counsellor trained to understand grief and the concerns related to death by suicide – can be of benefit to all of you. Evaluate your progress along with your counsellor to decide when you no longer need his or her support.

When people ask about your spouse and you don't know what to say, the following replies may help you. Say more if you want, but these responses allow you to say as little as possible and still be polite.

You: "He killed himself" or "She committed suicide."

They: "How did it happen?" or "What exactly happened?"

You: "I would rather not talk about it. I hope you understand" or "My husband shot himself. He must have felt he couldn't go on any more" or "My wife was depressed for a long time – she killed herself. She used her sleeping pills."

8. Death of a missing person.

If your spouse is a missing person, you will hope for a while that your husband or wife is not dead and all will be well. But as time passes and searches are unsuccessful, the grief reaction will set in. And eventually you will believe he or she is dead. Holding a special memorial service may help you and your relatives and friends to accept the death.

Months or years later when the body is found, you will grieve again but for a much shorter time than your original grief unless, of course, you did not believe your spouse was dead. If you had been hoping continuously that he or she would be found alive, you will be deeply affected by the evidence to the contrary, and you will now go through the entire grief process from shock to adjustment. You will see pictures in your mind of how he or she died. Try to think about the fact that he or she is no longer suffering.

There are factors other than those discussed here which can also complicate your progress through the grief process. Many people are faced with several critical situations at the same time. It will take longer to adjust under these circumstances.

2
Dealing with Your Feelings

Once you get through the initial shock and disbelief, you start to "thaw out" and feel again. Strong emotions emerge. You feel sad, of course, and sometimes very depressed. You feel anxious, angry, afraid and panicky. You feel a longing for the person who has died. Often you feel guilt for something left undone or things you wish you hadn't done. Sometimes there is a feeling of relief when someone dies who has been ill for a long time.

Grief responses include the following: not being able to think clearly, a show of hostility towards people (no one can do anything right for you), and expressing anger when comforters show concern ("Oh, leave me alone, let me do what I want" or "How do you think I feel?").

Anger

This is an important emotion in grief. Anger is a healthy reaction and one which most people have. Some people suppress it – that is, they won't admit to being angry because it seems inappropriate.

You may be angry at the person who died because he or she left you to face life alone. Sometimes you don't know why you are angry. A widow often feels certain people haven't done what they "should" have done or haven't lived up to her expectations – a doctor, the funeral director, the lawyer settling the estate, her children or her relatives. Is this justified? Sure, occasionally someone hasn't been kind or done the job they should have. Mostly, however, widowed people are angry at their circumstances, which are pretty hard to be angry at, because there is nothing to grab onto and no one to yell at or accuse.

Sometimes you are angry at God, too, feeling that he let you down by allowing your husband or wife to die in spite of your prayers.

One way of dealing with anger is to write or talk to the person who disappointed you. Write to your doctor, for example, or go and see him, if you think he should have been there but wasn't. You could also talk to someone else – a professional outsider, who might help you get rid of this anger.

Below are some of the feelings widows and widowers have told us they experienced. Describing feelings is not easy, but some of the words they used are: *empty, lost, angry, hurt, resentful, sad, unhappy, alone, lonely, unable, a failure, disappointed, isolated, in limbo, helpless, hopeless, waiting, irritable, restless, unfair, droopy, housebound, tired, exhausted, ruined, insecure, vague, useless, anxious, inactive, in a nightmare, apprehensive, uneasy, listless, weary, fearful, finished, stagnant, apathetic, self-pitying, guilty, in a dream, sensitive, vulnerable, easily hurt, remembering, suffering, thinking, cheated, unfulfilled, empathetic, dull, aimless, like half a person, feeling tummy tightness, weepy, worried, heartache, forgetful, sorry, unreal, if only I had known ... what if ... perhaps if ... I could have ... I didn't say good-bye, maybe if I had ... why us? why me? why her? why him? what's going to happen to me? if only we had been a bit older, if only he hadn't ... if only we hadn't ... if only we had ... I wish I hadn't ... how long will I feel this bad? how can I go on? it's hard learning to live without him, it's not fair, give me one good reason to go on without her, they tell me to snap out of it – how can I?*

Some people feel like screaming when they are angry, but worry that the neighbors will hear. One widow screams in the shower. Other ways to let off anger are to write about it – start a journal or write a letter and tear it up – or punch pillows or twist towels.

Talking may not be enough to get rid of your anger; it may only fuel it. If you talk to a friend who says you must take court action or that you are making everything up, you can end up feeling more angry and even less effectual and loyal to your spouse. Avoid situations like this, which only make you feel worse.

Anger can become depression if you turn it inward, so let it out in an acceptable manner. Run, walk fast, hammer that fence, and work off your anger. Then look into the substance of your charges – see if you really do have grounds to lay charges or write a critical letter to a professional organization about the treatment you or your spouse received. Don't stew over something you can do something about.

Do it. But remember, worrying over over what can't be changed is a waste of your time and energy.

Oversensitivity

Irritability is a common feeling in the early part of bereavement. You may find yourself unduly sensitive to what are usually judged to be small slights or insignificant actions.

If you have always been sensitive – inclined to interpret people's remarks as personal affronts – it might be appropriate at some time to change that attitude by attending a course or workshop on building self-esteem. However, if you are usually not so thin-skinned, it is due to your grief.

- Ask the person what he or she meant. You may have misunderstood.
- If it's an action or behavior that bothers you, point it out and ask for an explanation. People can't know that their actions irritate you unless you tell them.
- If it's a service person or someone who doesn't know you, remember that he or she doesn't know how you are feeling or what you've been through.

You may also find yourself feeling unusually short-tempered. Being short-changed by accident at your local drug store elicits a response of "Well, I'll never shop there again!" The lady ahead of you at the supermarket has a cheque to cash and it slows down the line (as usual); you pull your cart from the queue and stomp out of the store, grumbling about the inconsideration of "some" people, even though you know it is common practice for that supermarket to cash customers' cheques.

Minor irritations happen many times during the day, but they are usually taken in stride. You cope with the unexpected and with exasperating situations or people. While grieving, however, you become super-sensitive; situations you could normally handle with ease – acting as peacemaker to the neighborhood children and confidant to a friend whose wife is dying of cancer, or enduring the quarrelling of the next-door neighbors – all seem impossible now.

We can assure you that this oversensitivity will pass.

Avoiding the truth

Some people find it difficult to say "dead," so instead they say, "gone," "passed away, " "left." It's hard to say whether they think it is rude to be direct, or whether they hope that euphemisms make death less final. The truth is that he or she *is* dead and euphemisms can't change that. It can help you to believe it if you say "dead," "death" and "died" from the start.

Tears

Tears are a release to some people. If you don't feel like crying, this doesn't mean you aren't grieving naturally. For most people, however, crying is healthy. The tears can express anger, frustration, sadness or regret for something not said or done during marriage.

We talk about crying as "breaking down" and laughing as "breaking up," but both are just expressing your feelings. Crying can leave you feeling relieved and better able to go on. If you don't cry, and holding back the tears brings a "lump" in your throat or tightness in your abdomen, you feel even worse. If you start to cry in the company of people who are disturbed by your tears, you can say you'll be all right in a minute and explain, or you can excuse yourself and leave the room until you regain your composure.

Depression

The depression that is part of grief is called "reactive," meaning that you are depressed because of your loss and that this depression will gradually recede, along with your other grief reactions. It is characterized by a feeling that you don't want to do anything or go anywhere. You may have a tight feeling in your solar plexus, a "lump in your throat," and a general feeling of inertia. You may wake up at four o'clock in the morning with an overwhelming feeling of despair.

Even after you begin to adjust, depression can be retriggered by special dates (anniversary of the death, your spouse's birthday, holidays) or other reminders of your spouse. However, this reaction does not usually last long.

If you were subject to depression before the death of your spouse, you may need professional help.

Sadness

Of course you will be sad. Sadness and depression are not exactly the same but can be similar.

Some people are naturally more cheerful than others; some are quieter, more soft-spoken and a little more moody. Some widows have said, "I've always been a depressed person." A woman like this will probably never become a bubbly, energetic person after the death of her husband, but there is no reason to believe that she won't grieve naturally. Too often, well-meaning friends try to change someone's whole personality – encouraging them to return to a cheerfulness they never had – without knowing this is what they are doing.

Fears

Many widowed people have unfamiliar fears.

You have had fears of one kind or another before, but now there may be others – fear of being alone, fear of not being able to make it on your own, and fear that you will never feel better. Some widows and widowers are afraid they are going crazy. They think they see the person who has died – see him sitting in his chair, hear her coming up the stairs or just have the feeling that he's around. This is a normal reaction and does not mean they are losing their grip on reality.

You may also have a fear of inadequacy or of being unable to handle day-to-day problems. You will gradually regain your confidence; as time passes you see yourself managing in spite of the difficulties.

Lack of vitality

Lack of vigor in the early phases of grief often derives from your anxiety about what is going to happen to you and from tension and shock. It is temporary – you won't always feel this way. You will regain your vitality as you work through your grief.

Frustration

You may often feel helpless because you don't know what to do next. Waiting for probate to be finished is frustrating because you don't know what will change, how much money you will have, whether it will be enough and whether or not you will have to move. Naturally you want everything to be settled. You feel weary and anxious. You don't want to do anything prematurely. You often think it's taking too long to begin feeling better.

Another frustration is the feeling that nobody understands. Friends and family who have not faced such a loss may not know what you are going through. And you may not give relatives, friends and co-workers a chance to listen and help.

"If only . . ."

In the days and weeks following the death, you may think that everything would have been fine "if only" certain things had happened or not happened, "if only" you did or did not do certain things. You may feel bombarded by these thoughts. They are part of the grief process as you review your life and marriage and how your spouse died.

Look at your "if onlys" in perspective, if you are still bothered by them now. After you have re-examined these worrisome events, and perhaps talked them over with someone, you will begin to realize that there is nothing you can do now to change what happened. If you can accept your past efforts as what you felt was appropriate at the time, you will feel a great sense of relief from guilt and regret.

Typical "if onlys" which express feelings
of regret and perhaps guilt:

- If only she hadn't drunk so much, driven home, gone to . . .,
- If only it hadn't happened now, happened before retirement, happened so soon after we retired.
- If only we hadn't separated, hadn't argued, hadn't been away from each other, had said good-bye, had talked about it.
- If only he had eaten properly, taken his pills, been more careful, gone on that trip he always wanted.
- If only we had had children, hadn't had children, retired earlier, changed jobs sooner.
- If only she hadn't worried so much. If only she had gone to the doctor.
- If only she had stopped work sooner. If only he had kept on working.

Loneliness

Your loneliness comes from missing that most important person in your life. You are lonely wherever you are. You are lonely in groups; you are lonely by yourself; you are just lonely, period. As you adjust, the loneliness which has to do with your spouse will gradually diminish, and you will be able to find comfort in the company of other people. Your life will become more interesting and varied so that the gap will be filled to some extent. Of course this requires effort on your part, and some of the suggestions in this book can help you get started.

Another aspect of loneliness is a sense of isolation, which results from feeling misunderstood. There may be no one around who really understands how you feel. A support group of widowed people can be an immense help here. Members of such groups say, "I don't feel so alone anymore. I know other people are experiencing the same things." Call your local library or health centre to find out if there is a support group in your area. (In Appendix G we tell you how L.I.F.E. Resource Centre was started, and give suggestions on forming self-help support groups.)

A danger in feeling isolated is withdrawing and spending too much time by yourself. What is "too much" varies with the individual, of course, but if you are spending much more time alone than you did before, we suggest that you push yourself into extra activities, or get help by talking it over with someone. Tell him or her that you are feeling more and more isolated instead of less and less, as usually happens when grievers begin to adjust. Accept help when it is offered.

We can't tell you how long this strong feeling of loneliness will go on, but if you think your loneliness is lasting too long for you, and is affecting the way you function – then you need to do something about it. You have to reach out, look for interesting (and at first they may not seem as interesting as you'd like them to be) things to do, or try something new. Some people had interests or hobbies they let go when they married because their spouse wasn't interested or there wasn't time. Get back to the painting or sculpting or badminton or bowling that you once enjoyed. See if you can come up with something you might like to try again.

Most communities have centres you can phone or visit for suggestions and help. Although it may be difficult, make that initial phone call to a friend or an agency and be ready to accept the help they offer – an invitation to a talk, to go to her place for coffee, to hear a lecture or play tennis on Saturday morning. Getting out with other people will ease your long-term loneliness, if not your immediate loneliness.

"Stuck" in the grief process

Some widowed men and women continue to set an extra place at the table for months, even years. This indicates that they are "stuck" in the grief process and have not accepted the death.

Keeping treasured mementoes and pictures and placing them where you can see them does not mean you are stuck in your grief. If you look at them with pleasure, you are probably facing your loss and adjusting.

Looking back on your marriage

Looking back on your marriage is an essential part of your grief work. A good relationship will be reviewed with sadness at first, but with good feelings as you begin to adjust. If your relationship with your spouse was unsatisfactory, it may be painful to face the fact that your marriage was not what you'd hoped for.

Some widowed people tend to put the spouse on a pedestal, forgetting that he or she was not perfect. They attribute to him traits, some of which he had and some of which they wish he had, forming an idealized image.

If you find yourself pretending like this, don't be alarmed. This is a common phenomenon, and it often takes a while to be able to face the reality of your life with your spouse.

Friends and relatives often don't understand why and how a person whom they knew as human and imperfect has suddenly become perfect in death. They don't realize that the griever has idealized the spouse as a way to look back without guilt so that all the memories can be beautiful.

One indicator that you are moving ahead in the grief process is when you are willing to admit that your spouse had faults, that she wasn't perfect, that your relationship wasn't perfect and that you didn't always agree. It is a sign of real progress when you can see your relationship the way it was.

To help you reach this point, answer some of the questions in Marriage Review at the end of this chapter.

Often, insensitive friends or relatives will predict or suggest another marriage for you. One of the most inappropriate things said to newly widowed people is, "You are still young [or "still attractive"] and you can get married again." This hurts very much, as it shows no understanding of your love for and attachment to your dead husband or wife, which you feel very strongly. You are not ready to think about remarriage.

Your children may be concerned that you will remarry, and they need reassurance that you don't intend to remarry at present. Do not promise you will never remarry. You may be tempted to say so, but it is certainly unwise to make such a long-term promise.

If you had a very short marriage, people may say, "Oh, he won't be grieving, he's only lived with her for a little while." If the marriage was a rich experience for you, if you were close, if you shared interests and adventures for two, three, five years, it is an extremely traumatic loss.

If you've lived together for a long time, the adjustment period will be difficult. After living with someone for thirty or forty years, it seems unreasonable to expect that you will adjust to your new situation in one, two or perhaps three years. It will take time to learn to live without that person who has for so long been a part of your life.

If this was your second marriage, you may have experienced the death of a spouse before, although usually in different circumstances. The first time, for example, you may have been a young mother with children at home, while this time you are on your own. You may well find the two experiences quite different. We are often told by widows that with the second loss, one difference is that you don't have the children to think about and plan for. Now that you are older, it may seem more difficult to pick up your life, decide what to do and learn how to live alone. Your motivation will come from your sense of purpose and interest in your activities.

Unsatisfactory marriage

When people talk to a griever, you'll occasionally hear, "Well, at least you had a happy marriage."

This is not always a safe assumption. If you cannot look back on a satisfactory relationship with your wife or husband, you may be feeling additional guilt and remorse. You may believe you could have done something to improve your situation; you might even be burdened with a conviction that whatever went wrong was all your fault. You may wish most fervently to be able to go back and live it all again so that you could behave differently.

Remember that it takes two to make a relationship. He or she would have had to want to change, too; you did what you felt you could.

You may take a while to let go of these feelings, longer perhaps than someone who considered his or her marriage a good one.

Death of a former spouse

Don't be surprised if you feel grief when your ex-husband or ex-wife dies. You already went through a period of grief and recovered (we hope) when you divorced, but it would be natural for some of those feelings to recur. You may find yourself reviewing your time spent together and feeling some regret and sadness. This will probably last for only a short time. If it lasts longer than a few days or weeks, talk it over with a trusted friend or professional, perhaps a psychologist, psychiatrist or grief counsellor.

A grief reaction is likely even if you are remarried. It may help your present spouse to understand this if he or she realizes that your grief has nothing to do with your present relationship; it is a brief return to the past.

You may want to talk to someone other than your spouse about your feelings, as you may have to review your past relationship and this could be uncomfortable for your present husband or wife.

Memories

Memories can be very mixed, especially when you are first bereaved. Some of your memories hurt – even the good memories hurt at first. You no longer have that special person to reminisce with and it hurts so much to know that you will never share a memory with your spouse again.

You may even cut off your memories if you find them too painful, deciding not to look back at all.

You will need to look back at some time in order to progress through your grief, as reviewing your life together is part of your grief work.

Later on, your good memories will surface more and more. Friends and especially your children will appreciate remembering with you. They are likely to say, "Remember when . . .?" They seem to derive great pleasure from talking over the good times. Sharing those memories brings you closer together as a family.

Disturbing Memories

The degree to which your memories disturb you will depend a great deal on the circumstances of the death and, of course, on you.

These memories retrigger feelings of guilt (as mentioned earlier) or fear, as in the case of someone who was present when his or her partner died violently or accidentally. Flashbacks of the whole episode may be so vivid that it is like living it all again.

If these intrusive recollections are interfering with your ability to cope with your work and home life, consider getting help from a trained grief therapist.

Here are a few methods of dealing with mental pictures that recur at especially inappropriate times. The idea is to use another image to replace the intrusive memory.

1. Choose from your memory bank a picture, a time that gave you particular pleasure. This could be a childhood memory, or an actual photo of you with a friend, brother, sister, or parents involved in enjoyable activity.

   Look at a framed picture that gives you a feeling of serenity or look out your window if the view evokes a sense of peace.

   Read a poem that gives you comfort.

2. If you are in bed when you have the flashback, sit up and turn on the light. You might even say "Stop!" out loud. Then, if you have decided on an actual picture, have it on the bedside table, pick it up and look at it intently until your feelings become relaxed and peaceful.

If you are used to conjuring up mental pictures, this will be fairly easy. However, if this is a new idea to you, you may even find it hard to believe it is possible. (Close your eyes and count the windows in your living room and kitchen. Most people immediately "see" windows.)

Your flashbacks may occur while you are driving. By concentrating on the make and color of the car in front of you, or on other details such as the licence number, you will keep your mind focussed on the present.

If you are riding on the bus, switch to your pleasant memory, picture, poem, thought. And if the disturbing memory recurs, switch again or look out the window or listen to the conversation around you.

Recurring memories that elicit feelings of guilt can be dealt with using the approaches described above. Another helpful exercise is to list all the "good" things you have done in the past in relation to your spouse.

A distressing mental image often mentioned by grieving people is the memory of how the spouse looked in the last days of his or her illness. If that is your disturbing memory, imagine your mate when she or he was doing something he or she liked to do; find a snapshot in which she or he is laughing and happy. Again, make the substitution and concentrate on it until the unpleasant memory fades.

Marriage Review

At the Beginning

- When did you first meet your spouse? In what circumstances?
- What was he or she like when you first met? What attracted you to him or her? Did you dislike each other at first?
- How old were you both?
- What was your dating and courting like?

Marriage

- How soon after meeting did you marry?
- What kind of wedding did you have? Who was there?
- What did your relatives think of your marriage? What did your relatives think of your spouse?
- What did your in-laws think of you?
- What did your in-laws think of your marriage?

- What did your friends think of your marriage?
- What was your first home like?
- What did your spouse do best? What was the hardest?
- In what ways did marriage change your life?
- What was life like in the early days of your marriage?
- Where did you live? Was it hard to get by? How did you make a living?

Activities

- What did you do on vacations?
- How did you celebrate special family occasions?
- What kind of problems did you have in the early years of your marriage? How did you handle them?
- What holidays had special meaning? What preparations and events took place?

Children

- How did your spouse react to the birth of your first child?
- How did you and your spouse choose the childen's names?
- How did the children change your marriage? Your life?
- What values did you try to teach your children – religious, cultural, moral, social, family traditions?
- Why didn't you have children?
- Why didn't you have more children?
- What was your spouse like with the children when they were young? When they were older? When they were adults?

About Your Spouse

- How would you describe your spouse's personality? What kind of disposition did your spouse have? Mild? Patient? Volatile? Excitable? Quiet?
- How did your spouse show displeasure? To you? To the children? To others?
- How did your spouse show pleasure? To you? To the children? To others?
- What made your spouse laugh? Did you laugh at the same things?

- How did your spouse handle illness in the family?
- Did your spouse work during the last two years? What kind of work?
- What well-known people (political leaders, entertainment stars, sports figures) did your spouse admire and talk about?
- How did your spouse like to dress?
- What did your spouse enjoy doing on his or her own?
- Who was your spouse's best friend?
- What was your spouse's favorite food?
- What did your spouse like to do whenever there was free time?
- Where did your spouse like to go often?
- What was your spouse's worst disappointment?
- What ability did your spouse have that he or she was very proud of?
- What about work in the house and yard - was your spouse capable and helpful?
- How did your spouse deal with problems? How did he or she react to being between jobs?
- Who did your spouse consult with when decisions had to be made?

You and Your Spouse

- Name some of the places you have lived since your marriage.
- What sorts of things did you and your spouse enjoy together?
- What kind of a marriage partner was your spouse?

You

- What was your ordinary day like? What was a fun day like? What happened to make a day unpleasant?
- How did you deal with problems?
- What did you do when a child was ill?
- How did you react to being between jobs?
- Who did you consult with when decisions had to be made?
- What did you enjoy doing with a friend or with others (without your spouse)?

- What did you enjoy doing on your own?
- What exercise did you like? (aerobics, team sports, skiing, walking, running?)

As you deal with the emotional and physical aspects of grief, there are specific things you can do to keep some order in your life.

Touching

Touching is something we miss when a spouse dies; it is a need that is no longer met. You may wish to ask friends and relatives to touch you or hug you. But this isn't for everybody.

If you are trying to help a new widow and she draws away when you touch her, she probably doesn't like to be touched by strangers or in certain circumstances. However, some widows and widowers are comforted by having an arm put around them or by holding hands.

Sexual feelings – what do you do with them?

In the first months of your bereavement, you may not even think about or miss the sexual part of your relationship with your spouse. As you begin to adjust, however, you may realize how much you miss your sex partner. This depends on whether or not you have had an active sexual relationship. Some couples have had to be satisfied with touching, hugging and kissing because of illness.

There are many ways of dealing with these feelings when they surface, and some will suit you better than others. The following are some of the approaches widowed men and women have found helpful:

"I think all these feelings are part of energy, so I get busy and scrub the floor and clean like crazy."

"I ask for hugs from my children and grandchildren, and that seems to help."

"My husband was ill for so long that I got used to settling for hugs and kisses. We had such a wonderful relationship otherwise that it didn't really matter. Right now, it's no problem because I have so many friends and my family, too."

"My children think I'm too old at 60 to have sex, but I do. For a year after my wife died I did some dating which sometimes included sex, but I didn't have a serious relationship till recently."

"It doesn't bother me too much because I couldn't have sex without love."

"I am grateful now that I don't have a strong sex drive."

"I stay away from erotic films and literature and I hardly ever think about it."

"Right after my wife died I felt guilty about wanting sex, but now I know it's normal."

Some people are able to relieve the feelings temporarily by masturbation. Others find a lover with whom to fulfill their needs for a sexual relationship. Still others find celibacy the only choice for them. Of course, you have your own values and make up your own mind about what you want to do.

All forms of exercise can help to disperse and use sexual tension – a brisk walk, swim or game of tennis – and there's always the cold shower.

Some ways of handling sexual feelings can be disruptive in the long run. Some grievers have formed sexual alliances with strangers or people they would never have associated with at any other time in their lives. Looking back, they realize they'd gone a little crazy in their desire to satisfy their need for love and affection.

Later, when their ability to think clearly returned, they were faced with the necessity of ending these relationships and dealing with the accompanying guilt feelings of having betrayed their own values.

You will feel most comfortable following your own personal beliefs regarding sexual behavior.

Your health

The newly bereaved person should make the effort to stay healthy. There is a tendency to skip meals, especially if you are living alone. You don't feel like cooking; you don't feel like eating; you don't feel like going out to shop. Studies have shown that your immune system is adversely affected by grief, so you are doubly at risk if you don't take particular care to protect your health.

Your doctor will probably suggest that you have a check-up. If you are anxious about your health, make an appointment as soon as possible.

Although recently doctors have become more aware of the needs of widowed people, many are still very uncomfortable with their grieving patients. If your doctor is unwilling to talk with you about your feelings or to listen to your concerns, this may be a good time to change doctors.

Visiting your doctor

- Take with you a list of questions and concerns you wish to talk about.
- Find out how much time the doctor is willing to spend with you. (A doctor usually spends five to twenty minutes with a patient in an office.) If you have a lot to say or ask about, request several appointments or ask the doctor for suggestions. He or she may prefer that you talk with a nurse, social worker, counsellor or specialist.

Exercise daily

Exercise is one of the most beneficial things you can do. It will help maintain your health throughout your grieving process, and can ease some of the tension and give you extra strength and energy.

Whatever physical activity you enjoy will be the best one for you. If you already have an exercise routine, continue it. If not, begin one.

Walking is an excellent form of exercise, and is well-suited to those who have not been exercising regularly. Before beginning any exercise program, however, it is important that you check with your doctor.

Whether you walk, ride a bike, skate, swim, jog or skip – get some physical exercise every day. You'll feel better for it.

Meals for widowed people

Cooking

Some widowed people are not used to cooking their own meals. When you are newly bereaved, you may not feel like learning those things immediately, so eating in a restaurant at least once a day will keep you going until you master some basics.

If you do not feel like eating three regular meals a day, eat nutritious snacks six or seven times a day. Whip up an eggnog, for example – it's nutritious and doesn't take very long. Raw vegetables, fruit and cheese are other good suggestions. Watch that you don't fill up on junk food. Instead, go to the fast-food section of your store and buy anything that tempts you.

You may find it helpful to attend a cooking class. You are likely to make new friends as well as learn how to cook. Once you learn a few kitchen skills you will feel more independent, and you will be pleased to find that you are able to create even gourmet dishes.

Grocery shopping
- Make a list and take it with you.
- Buy yourself a treat. If you love avocados, for instance, buy one even though it is out of season.
- Make sure you buy nutritious food for a balanced diet. It's especially important to eat well at this time.
- Shop every day to get you out of the house or away from your work place, and so that you don't have an excuse to just snack because you've run out of food.
- Go with specific purchases in mind.

Waiting

Often for months and even occasionally years after the death of a spouse, the griever endures the waiting game with impatience – waiting for the funeral, waiting for the estate to be settled, waiting for pensions to begin, waiting for grief to subside, waiting for the court case to be over.

There isn't much you can do to shorten this waiting time, but perhaps you can develop an attitude towards it that minimizes the worry and stress.

Court cases are particularly hard because you must relive the intense emotions and repeat over and over the details of what happened. You feel you can't get on with your own life until the court case is finished, and it is difficult to live day by day in limbo.

Be active while you are waiting. Try to enjoy a portion of every day so that you are controlling your life, not being controlled by the person or thing that is making you wait.

Familiar things

Familiar things give comfort. If you are able to stay in a familiar environment, you will probably manage better than if you move to a new area and lose touch with the neighborhood and people you are used to seeing every day – the letter carrier, milkman or people at your corner grocery store.

Keeping to your regular routine helps, too, even though you may wonder why you are doing it – for whom? why? who cares? But continuing with usual activities does help, because it gives you a sense of security while adjusting. So make the beds and vacuum if you are used to doing these things, go to work, tend the garden and walk the dog.

Balancing your day

At times when you feel you are doing too much and you want to slow down, the following hints may be useful in establishing a temporary balance in your day. Set aside the time you need for less hectic living by creating some oases in your schedule and some changes of activity.

If you always feel too hurried:

- Walk a few blocks on your usual route but return a different way. Look at what's new or changing in your neighborhood.
- Put your feet up and have a snooze.
- Browse through old magazines, sorting them into two piles for reading and throwing out, but stopping to read interesting articles and looking at the photographs as you go, with no time limit.
- Watch TV for no other reason than relaxing.
- Listen to a long-playing record.
- Needlepoint a cushion cover a few inches at a time.
- Chat with a friend on the phone.
- Think about an activity you enjoy – playing golf, working on your hobby, sleeping in on Sunday morning.
- Decide to have a fun activity at least once a day, even if it lasts for only half an hour.
- Rent a video machine and a comedy film.
- Read a funny or light-hearted book.

You may have a hard time getting around to what you feel you should do or have promised to do. Learn to make time for everything that is important to you and the family, both at work and at leisure.

If you work outside the home, consider these suggestions:

- Before going to work, make a list, planning the chores you need to do when you get home.
- Plan to skip some of your regular routine activites so you can fit in the "something" you feel would be real luxury.
- When planning your work or day, include some pleasurable activities along with the essential.
- Remind yourself that you need this job, money, experience or instruction.

- Remember that you want a raise or promotion.
- Remember that you always get enthusiastic once you are at work, even though you may not feel like going now.

When you think you "should" be doing a specific activity but would rather be doing something else, decide if it really is necessary to do the "should" item or whether it can wait for later.

If it can't wait but you are still hesitating or procrastinating, perhaps one of the following suggestions will help to motivate you:

- Imagine how good it will feel when the job is finished.
- Remember the enthusiasm you had when you decided to do the task originally. What made you consider doing the activity – money, prestige, friends, job, something to talk about to your friends and family, it is educational, fun?
- Think how useful the result will be.
- Decide to spend five minutes on it. This might create enough momentum to make a sizeable dent in the job at hand.
- Make a game of the task to start with. Maybe you'll enjoy it.

Flexibility

Some bereaved people are more upset than usual by inconveniences, thoughtlessness, and minor disruptions.

Things will always crop up unexpectedly in your day-to-day affairs, requiring you to make changes. Some people think this means they are incompetent, or that others are incompetent or unreliable. Although this is sometimes true, it is really just the way things are. Humans make mistakes and machines malfunction; departments make changes in policy but you don't find out until you get to the wrong wicket; and employees don't know all the answers so you may be referred elsewhere.

Be prepared to accept a certain amount of inconvenience and imperfection. Have a few contingency plans ready that will work for the most common inconveniences, even if you can only think of two or three, such as: ask questions, stop what you're doing and try to think of another option, or relax for a moment.

When someone fails to show up on time for an appointment, when your car won't start, when the garburator breaks down just before your family Sunday dinner – don't feel trapped. You could leave a note saying you were there on time and have now gone home (with your conscience clear); call the automobile association or a tow truck for your car or take a bus or taxi; stop stuffing things down the garburator and use another sink and then laugh it off with your family when they arrive (someone may even know how to unplug it).

When the unexpected happens, stop for a moment and consider your options. There are often more than you might think at first. When the family comes for supper unannounced and you are not willing, for whatever reason, to prepare a meal, suggest that you all go out for dinner Dutch treat. If you wish to join them, fine, but if not you can say so, as nice as it was of them to think of you and drop over. You could suggest that they go out to eat without you and come back for coffee. You could offer to treat them to a meal at the local coffee shop down the block. Then, when it seems appropriate, you could suggest that a phone call next time would suit you better than a surprise visit.

Happiness

No one is happy all the time. All your life there are moments of happiness and moments of sadness.

Widowed people sometimes feel very depressed or sad, but when asked if they felt like that before, during their marriage, they admit that there were times of sadness and depression even then.

Put it in perspective. Happiness is not something we can count on. We have ups and downs. If you are usually optimistic, you will adjust more quickly than a person who has a negative point of view. Not that a person with a negative view can't be changed. If you consider yourself a pessimistic person, you can still turn your negative thoughts into positives.

How can I be happy at a time like this, you might ask. You can if you are willing to set your grief aside for a few minutes in order to enjoy something – reading, going somewhere or being with someone you like.

Happiness means different things to different people. It can mean having a cup of tea with a neighbor; watching birds fly; seeing spring flowers coming into blossom; a hug from a friend; a family who loves you; reading an interesting book; being absorbed in a favorite activity.

Sometimes you may feel guilty and disloyal to your spouse when you laugh and enjoy yourself with friends. Why? Because your spouse is not there to have a good time too? Because you suddenly realized you laughed or smiled and for a while forgot how sad and numb you are so often? Or are you afraid of what people might think if you smile and joke occasionally and begin to feel your old self again?

Laughter eases tension, and it can be reassuring to know you have not lost your sense of humor. Welcome these moments of joy as a respite from your overwhelming feelings of grief. See them as signs of hope for the future – that eventually you will be able to enjoy your life in spite of your loss.

For widowers

Your needs and concerns are different in some ways, and age also seems to make a difference.

Older widowers have often been accustomed to having their wives handle the house, bills and social arrangements with family and friends. Of these, social events seem to be the most difficult to handle. The widower often feels left out of things. Learning to cook, clean or make financial arrangements are not all that hard, but dealing with Auntie, organizing a dinner party and knowing what to give the grandchildren for Christmas are not skills you can acquire in one fell swoop – they take time. Friendships, even with relatives and family, are cultivated over time.

You may also find it hard to ask for help with these problems and concerns. Men sometimes have difficulty asking for help because they think they are supposed to be able to handle everything themselves. Men do not often confide their feelings to each other in the way women do, and this may make it more difficult to work through your grief.

Older men may be used to having someone at home when they return from work. They are not accustomed to being alone or on their own for any length of time. The empty house is a particular problem, especially in the early months.

Being responsible for young children for the whole evening after the sitter or housekeeper has gone home, listening to their chatter and problems and getting them to bed can be a difficult adjustment for you if your wife usually looked after them. The normal strain between parent and teenager is magnified many times by the death of a parent, and surviving fathers may find this especially hard to handle.

Children who are not used to being left with their father find everything changed and feel utterly lost at first. Their adjustment, as well as their father's, will depend partly on what the father-child relationship was like before the mother died.

Age

The "mature" student is no longer a novelty on college campuses, where students in their 80s and 90s are working toward degrees or auditing courses.

If you are in your 50s or 60s and think you are too old to go to school, start a career or start a business, or acquire new interests – older people than you have done exciting new things in their middle and later years. You can, too.

Procrastination and excuses

You will reach a point where you are living more in the present than in the past and you become interested in plans for the future. Is it possible that you are keeping yourself from doing the things you would like to do by using "if only" as an excuse? Are any of the phrases below things you tell yourself and your friends?

> *Procrastination phrases – "if onlys" – that prevent the griever from getting on with life as a widow, widower, single person, or single mother or father:*
> If only I wasn't alone, a woman, a mother, so young, so old. If only I could learn, make, think of, get over, study ... If only I knew what to do, how to, someone who could, when to, where to go to. ...

Information and help

Information and help is available in your community or nearby. The fact is that you must make the first phone call or write the first letter, however difficult that may be. It is the first in a series of actions that will bring you to what you want to do and where you want to go.

Perhaps your first call would be to a friend who can make a suggestion. To get your information, you will need to make more phone calls, set up appointments, see people, perhaps buy something. Information-gathering is necessary for all your day-to-day needs – residence repairs, shopping, job-hunting, or babysitting. Yes, this is what you usually do, but you now have more things to handle than you used to – and all at once. Being emotionally drained just makes it harder to get at them all as quickly and perhaps as effectively as you would like.

If a business might have the answers you want, choose one from the appropriate section of the phone book and don't be afraid to ask "stupid" questions. It is in the company's best interest to be helpful and courteous. Take your inquiry (and business) elsewhere if you are not treated with respect.

Signs of adjustment

Adjusting to your new status is an ongoing process. Rarely would anyone go through this process without some overlapping of the stages we mention here.

- Sleeping and eating patterns returning to normal.
- Ability to concentrate improving.

- Weight stabilizing.
- Spending most of your time enjoying what you are doing now.
- You are more concerned with the present than with the past.
- Remembering your spouse as a person with characteristics you didn't like, as well as qualities you loved.
- Accepting your relationship with your spouse the way it was.
- Accepting the past the way it really was.
- Relinquishing guilt – knowing you did what you could and what seemed appropriate at the time.
- Disappointment replacing your anger at paid caregivers, relatives, well-meaning friends or your spouse.
- Planning your future with enthusiasm.
- Discovering coping skills you didn't know you had and appreciating your own ingenuity.
- Being willing to risk new activities and situations.
- Adopting a positive attitude towards life in general.
- Building new relationships.

Single again

Many false assumptions are made about how single people feel, especially by married people. Some of them think all single people are looking for someone to marry, that they are unhappy and unfulfilled and need a man or woman to make them feel whole again. You may want to find a new companion or you may enjoy living on your own. It is a personal choice.

Answering personal questions and acknowledging sympathy

There are several ways you can handle the curious or caring people who ask questions. You can practise these replies ahead of time, in front of a mirror even, so that you are prepared.

You: "My husband is dead. I'm a widow."

They: "What happened to him?"

You: "He had cancer" (or a bad heart, MS, etc.) or "It was an accident" or "She was murdered" or "We don't know exactly."

And if your spouse committed suicide, you might respond:

"He killed himself" or "She committed suicide."

If the person simply acknowledges the death of your spouse, perhaps expressing sympathy, you might reply, "Thank you for your concern. Yes, it is a hard time for me."

4
Letter Suggestions

Acknowledgments

Thanking people for their expressions of condolence – the cards, letters, gifts and kindnesses – is done within the first few months, the sooner the better. You can send them as you do them, or wait until you have the notes completed and send them all at once.

Sympathy letters will arrive up to a year later, as distant friends and acquaintances may not hear of the death until they inquire about you, wondering why they haven't heard from you for months or why they didn't receive a Christmas card.

You may cry and feel sad and glad all at once when you receive help, cards, letters and gifts meant to comfort from sympathetic friends, family and strangers. These gestures mean "we care about you" and "we cared about your spouse," reminding us that we are part of a family and a community and that we are respected and loved. Writing thank-you notes enables us to thank our well-wishers in a tangible way.

Mostly you will be cheered and comforted by the telegrams, cards and letters you receive. Keep them in a prominent place for a week or more, so that you can show them to family and friends.

Bereaved people often find acknowledging condolences – writing the notes and letters – one of the hardest parts of the grieving process and are always glad when they have finished the last letter.

Some grievers avoid meeting acquaintances and certain friends because acknowledgement letters haven't been sent yet. And a few grievers stop corresponding with friends and distant family for years because they didn't know how to reply to messages of condolence, and they feel embarrassed to resume their usual letter-writing when they haven't said, "Thank you for thinking of me when Bill died. I don't feel like writing letters right now, but as soon as I'm up to it, you will be the first to hear from me." Writing something like this at the time could have prevented much discomfort.

If you find yourself putting off writing these, remind yourself that this is part of your grief work, and you will definitely benefit from completing the acknowledgement notes.

Printed cards of thanks (available in stationery or department stores) are acceptable among all but the most traditional families today. However, if you think that someone might feel offended by a "commercial" card, you have a few choices. You can send it anyway and risk their comments (usually a grumbling that "one is supposed to write a note by hand"). You can send it, but write a line or two at the bottom to people you know quite well.

If your spouse was (or you are) a public figure and you receive hundreds of messages of condolence, custom-printed or engraved cards may be sent to people you don't know. If you are acquainted with some to whom you are sending engraved cards, add a short personal message as well as your signature.

The family of
John L. Smith
wishes to thank you for
your kind expression of sympathy

Mrs. Arthur Brown
gratefully acknowledges
your kind expression
of sympathy

Mr. Charles Crofton
expresses his grateful appreciation
of the sympathy of
. . . .
(write in the name of the person you are sending the
acknowledgement to)
in his bereavement

These cards, traditionally, are not sent to people who have sent flowers or to intimate friends and family who have written personal letters.

If your spouse was well-known, you may wish to place a notice in the newspaper:

*Mrs. B. Brown was deeply touched by the kind letters
and lovely flowers sent to her on her bereavement.
She will reply personally as soon as possible.*

Try not to dwell on expressions of sympathy that offend you or that you don't believe in. Think instead of the person who sent the card or letter – they probably thought they were doing what was "right" or what they would have appreciated were they the mourner. As you are especially sensitive now, remember you may feel different in a month or two and you will certainly not be as touchy and emotional about some of the sentiments written to you.

Hints and help

It is customary to send a note or letter even though it may be the same thank-you letter copied over and over, with just the salutation and closing varying (depending on how well you know the person your are writing to). A handwritten, personal message on a fold-over card or good-quality stationery is the preferred acknowledgement. You may wish to use blue ink, as it seems to be less jarring to the griever than black.

Don't feel obliged to reply to cards that haven't personal notes on them; you can put those aside. Then, tackle your acknowledgements of flowers (aided by the funeral director's notes on the kinds of flowers and names of senders), telegrams, notes and letters, donations to charities, Mass cards and personal assistance.

Set reasonable goals for yourself – write three thank-you notes a day, for example. This will help to keep you from feeling overwhelmed, and it will get the job done.

To save you time and effort – so that you can get on with it and get it over with – here are some useful sentences and phrases. Use them as they are, or reword them to create your own.

Dear Aunt Caroline,

I want you to know how much I appreciated your thoughtfulness and concern for me when Patricia died.

It is still difficult for me to write letters, so forgive this short note. I will write later on when I am less upset.

Please write in the meantime if you can spare the time.

Sincerely,

Dear Mrs. Jones,

It was kind of you to think of us at such a difficult time. Your spring flowers were beautiful.

Sincerely,

Dear Linda,

Your kind expression of sympathy was greatly appreciated, and the pink carnations comforted me. I cannot tell you how much your loving kindness has meant to me.

Love,

Dear Brian,

Thank you for all the help you gave me when George was ill. I really appreciated your thoughtfulness and assistance.

Sincerely,

Dear Elizabeth,

Thank you for thinking of us at this time. Your donation to the Heart Foundation is most appreciated.

I'll miss the class reunion this year but I will write later when I feel up to it.

Sincerely,

Dear Penny,

Let me thank you and Frank for your kindness. Your message of sympathy meant a great deal to me, and it touched me deeply that you remembered Martha's preference in the beautiful flowers you sent. Your friendship has always meant a lot to me.

With love,

Dear Mark,

It was very good to know you were thinking of me when Katherine died.

Thank you for your concern.

Sincerely,

If a friend or family member is helping you, he or she could write:

Joan asks me to thank you for your beautiful flowers and kind message of sympathy.

When you have finished your last note of acknowledgement, you will find yourself another step ahead in your progression through grief.

Business letters

Telephone your spouse's life insurance company, asking for the agent your spouse used if you know him or her. If you don't have the agent's name, give them your spouse's full name and any other information you are asked for. Even when you phone, you may be asked to send them the same information in a letter. Use the following letter as a guide. (If the lawyer settling the estate wants to do this for you, you may be charged for his or her time, for gathering the information you probably already know, and for follow-up letters and meetings with the insurance agent.)

Your address
Date
Their address
Dear (agent's name or Sir or Madam if you don't know it):

Further to our telephone conversation of _____(date you talked to them), *I am sending you the information you requested.* (If it is a document of some kind you are sending, photocopy it. If they insist on having the original, keep the photocopy for yourself until they return the original, register your letter and pay for a "return card" – this means the post office will send back this card so that you know the insurance company received your letter.)

Please send me whatever documents I will need to complete a claim under my husband/wife's policy – policy number _____. *My husband/wife,* _____(full name), *died on* _____(date).

Did my husband/wife have any other insurance coverage with your company?

Sincerely,

Other Insurance

Your address
Date
Their address

Dear Sir,

> *Regarding policy number* _____.
> *My husband/wife,* _____(full name), *died on* _____(date). *What steps should I take to maintain coverage on the car/house/cottage/boat/property?*
> *Please send me any forms that would be appropriate in my case.*

Sincerely,

Government pension plans (i.e. Canada Pension Plan, Quebec Pension Plan)

Your address
Date
Their address

Dear Sir,

> *My husband/wife,* _____(full name), *died on* _____(date). *His/her Social Insurance Number is* _____ (if you know. If you don't know it, leave the sentence out but try to find it from income tax files or his or her wallet.) *Please advise me what benefits are available and what other information you need.*

Sincerely,

Employer or past employers

Your address
Date
Their address

Attention: Personnel Manager
Dear Sir,

As you know, (if they have already been notified) *my husband/wife* _____ (full name) *died on* _____(date). *Please send the forms I need, as beneficiary, to apply for all the benefits provided by your company.*

Sincerely,

Part Two
Practical Matters

5
Legal and
Financial Considerations

You may find some of the points helpful in *What to Do when Someone Dies* compiled by Watt for the L.I.F.E. Resource Centre. We include them here because they touch on all the main aspects you have to deal with in the first two or three weeks.

What to do when someone dies – the practical matters*

At first

- When the death happens at home, call a doctor. He or she will tell you to call an ambulance or a funeral facility.
- When the death is at the hospital – someone will phone or come and tell you. The hospital will ask you to call a funeral facility.
- Before you contact a funeral director (if you are by yourself when you are told of the death) you should call a close family member or friend. Right now, you need family and friends; you want their help, comforting and sympathy.
- After you talk with your family members and friends and discuss funerals, *then* call a funeral facility. Take your time; you may need a whole day to think about this.
- If you are the executor review the will to see if there is something that has to be done immediately. Some wills contain burial instructions.
- If you are not the executor and know the location of the will and the name of the executor – contact him or her.

*© 1984 Jill Watt for L.I.F.E.
For permission to make copies, write to L.I.F.E. Resource Centre Society, #101, 395 W. Broadway, Vancouver, B.C. V5Y 1A7

Funeral Arrangements

If your spouse did not leave burial instructions or state any preferences, you will be asked to consider some of these things:

- embalming – yes or no.
- cremation – scattering or burial of ashes.
- cemetery – location, maintenance cost.
- service in church or hall, full funeral, memorial or no service. Casket lid open or shut.
- flowers or donations to charity
- time of service (usually within 10 days)
- cost of arrangements including special cars, music and obituary notices.

A Registration of Death to the Department of Statistics is required. This form is usually filled out by the funeral director who will ask you for the information. If you are not sure how to answer some questions say so, but reply to the best of your knowledge. The information wanted about the deceased is (1) name, home address and phone number (2) how long in the province (3) name of business, address and phone number (4) occupation and title (5) social insurance number (6) war veteran's serial number (7) date of birth (8) place of birth (9) Canadian citizen? (10) father's and mother's names (11) birthplace of parents (12) religious denomination, if any.

Arrange for help for family and house – for example, child care, house sitter during the funeral and reception, food ordering and housecleaning.

Notifying people about the death and funeral

Give people the opportunity to attend the service (by invitation only if you like), to acknowledge the death and extend sympathy to you and your family. Ask a friend or family member to help you.

People to notify:

- immediate family and relatives, near and far
- friends, executor of spouse's will, employer and work colleagues
- minister, church committee, clubs, service organizations, military (veteran association), school
- any person or group that the deceased person had an interest in – think of his or her job, hobbies, interests and volunteer work.

Arrange for money for now and the next few months. Open a bank account in your own name.

A few days later and after the funeral

- Notify the deceased's bank.
- If you are executor – open a bank account to handle the deceased's affairs. It will be in your name and you can use a different bank if you like but it should be handy for you. "In Trust" does not have to be indicated in the account name. You will require a lawyer or notary. A few widowed people do all the work themselves but unless the estate is very small and the will simple and straightforward we don't suggest you even try to settle the estate yourself. However, we recommend you read a Wills and Probate information book** so you know what others should be doing on your behalf when you hire them, e.g. lawyers and trust companies.

Helping the executor

- Documents: Collect all papers that look important. Check with him or her so you don't duplicate or omit things or tasks.
- Telephone or write the deceased's life insurance company. (There might be more than one policy and not necessarily with the same firm – check all policies, not just the latest one).
- Apply for pensions if applicable.
- Money owing: Check all debts and installment payments incurred by the deceased. Some may carry cancellation clauses. The executor makes contact with the creditors.

**Information on probate and the duties of the executor is available from most libraries, booksellers and stationery stores.

Helping yourself

- Income: Begin to collect information on the probable income for the survivor (you, we presume).
- Carefully consider your circumstances before changing your living accommodations. Get the estate settled and see what your income will be and give yourself time (12 to 14 months).
- Get in touch with your local community organization that helps bereaved people for information and ongoing emotional and practical support.
- Your own will may need to be revised. If you don't have a will, get one.

- Write thank-you and acknowledgment letters as soon as possible.

Help people help you

When people offer to help you, they will need some tools. One of the best is a list of phone numbers, including emergency numbers.

First on your list should be phone numbers for ambulance, doctor, fire department, and police. Write it down – don't expect anyone to remember phone numbers or addresses at this time of emergency and unhappiness.

If you hire a housekeeper, she will need phone numbers such as the cleaners, school office, your office number, your sister or father's phone number and the hardware store and department store where you have charge accounts. If she uses the car, she'll also need the service station phone number.

If friends help with the funeral arrangements, settling the estate, caring for the children, or helping out with your business, they will need additional phone numbers, such as your bank manager, lawyer and accountant, etc. (for more ideas for people and services to add to your personal phone list, see Appendix F.)

Legal help

If your spouse dies without a will, it's complicated and you will need expert legal advice.

If you are the major beneficiary but are not the executor or co-executor of your spouse's will, the settling of the estate is the job of the executors. You should insist on being kept informed on how things are progressing every week or so until probate is completed and the estate is settled. Some of the questions you need to have answered are:

- How will you obtain the money you need now to run the home or to live?

- How long does the executor think it will take to settle the estate and distribute the assets?

- What does he or she think the estate is worth and what does that mean exactly?

- Are property, pensions, insurance policies in your name or in that of the estate?

If you are the executor, the complications of estate settlement and the probate procedure usually require some legal help. Choose a lawyer who settles estates often. (Some lawyers spend most of their working lives in other types of legal work such as corporate law, divorce, or court cases.)

Find out what you can do yourself to reduce legal costs. Ask the lawyer what the fees will be and what the difference would be if you did some of the work yourself – for example, changing the car title or house title into your name (if you are entitled to do this).

Keep a record of the phone calls you make to the lawyer and the letters he writes on your behalf. Request an itemized bill. Photocopy the letters and documents you send to him so you have copies. In this way you can refer to your paper file when he or she phones you. Always keep a duplicate of the papers. Call the life insurance agent yourself if you are the beneficiary. You don't need a lawyer to call him to ask him to call you.

It is important to remember that the lawyer's time costs money, as casual as he or she may be – "Call me anytime" – so be prepared before you visit or make a phone call. List the questions you want answered and phone only if necessary after the first visit. Clarifying what you want to accomplish in that visit will shorten the time you need to spend with him or her.

Here is a list of the documents you need to take on your first visit to the lawyer if he or she doesn't already have them: will, burial plans, birth certificate, social insurance number (social security number), stocks, bonds, any financial papers such as bank books in your spouse's name, names and phone numbers of stockbrokers, loans officers, insurance agents and accountants who handled your spouse's affairs, insurance policies (especially those of fire and theft of properties that your spouse owned – so that the premiums can be kept up to date) and income tax information for the last year.

If your were wholly or partially dependent on your spouse's income

Many widows are faced with a change in income. You may have more money than you've ever had before; you may have less; you may have none; you may have the same amount. There may be debts that your spouse incurred which must be paid from the estate before it is distributed to the beneficiaries ("estate" means everything a person, whether alive or dead, owns – securities, money, property, antiques, car, personal effects).

You may be eligible for government social assistance; telephone your local Social Service department to find out. If you are not eligible, your minor children might be. It takes about six months to settle an uncomplicated estate.

Maybe your spouse handled the family finances and you were given an allowance. If so, a lump sum insurance payment can seem large. Often, however, it is not nearly enough to keep you going for the rest of your life if you were even partially dependent on your spouse's income. For instance, a $50,000 insurance payment might give you the illusion that you are rich, but only until you realize that invested at, say, 10%, you would have only $5,000 a year.

If you don't already have a financial advisor, your bank will give you basic information on term deposits and saving certificates. They will explain the difference between long-term and short-term deposits, the interest rates and also the terms that apply when you withdraw the funds ahead of the maturity date. Some bank certificates cannot be withdrawn before the maturity date. Clarify that before you invest. (For more information, see Appendix H for books on how to manage money.)

Your Financial Situation

The following chart will help you to get a clearer picture of your current and future financial status.

	Used to be	Is now	When estate is settled
Income			
• employment income			
• pensions			
• rental income			
• interest & dividends from investments			
• other			
Assets			
• stocks			
• bonds			
• bank certificates (term deposits)			
• real estate			
• other (e.g. vehicles, antique collection)			
Expenses			
• accommodation			

- utilities
- medical
- insurance
  (life, theft, fire)
- credit cards
- education
- transportation
- food
- clothes
- personal
- other

When asked for money

Don't jeopardize your financial future before you have all the facts. Tell children, relatives or anyone else who asks you for money, a donation or gift of cash that you have none to spare and you don't know when you may have.

6
Day-to-Day
Living

Accommodation

As a new widow or widower, stay where you are for a while if possible. Too many changes now will cause additional distress, and moving to an new home, district or town would be a big change. Resist the pressure from many well-meaning people to get you to move. Within weeks someone is bound to say, "That's a big house for you to be in all by yourself with no help. Where are you going to live?" Whether you are a man or woman, young or old, people seem to want you to move. Many single people live alone and manage a house and garden, yet when there is a death of a spouse there is always a professional or two, some family and friends, acquaintances and strangers, who assume you must or should move right away – that your residence is not suitable! In their opinion, of course.

Once you have been on your own for a year or two, you can reassess the situation. Perhaps you feel that the house is too big or too small, or you never liked it, or maintenance takes a lot of your time and you would rather do other things (expenses, for example, eat up all your cash and leave you unable to afford the tennis club). If so, then you can consider other accommodation. But take as long as you need to look for your next home. Don't allow anyone to press you into a quick move even then, because you need to assess carefully what will be best for you. Do you want an apartment or a townhouse? Should you buy or rent or share? Think of your family requirements in three- to five-year periods, considering your children's ages, schools, transportation and your work and leisure activities. Look at all the possibilities before you make your move.

On the other hand, if after a few years you are still living in the same home and like it and can afford it, keep it – there's no need to move at all. The decision is yours alone.

Finances may dictate that you move to a bachelor apartment or other inexpensive accommodation following your spouse's death. Try to keep as many things as possible the same. Stay in town if you are used to city living; look for a similar neighborhood, with familiar means of transportation; try to remain as near your friends and family as you are now.

If you must make an early move, recognize that this is another change which may add to your distress. Also, remember that circumstances change, and you don't necessarily have to remain at this new address forever. Then again, you may find that you like it after a while – it may require less maintenance, or the new neighborhood might be very much to your liking.

Sleeping

Go to bed when you feel tired, regardless of what the clock says.

If you are not tired:

- read (not in bed, but in your night clothes and after having locked up, put the cat out and done all those other before-bed tasks)
- watch TV
- sew, cook or bake
- change that dripping tap washer
- study something or review your language class lesson
- do *not* do any vigorous exercises
- eat a small amount of carbohydrates (small bowl of cereal, slice of bread or toast)

If you are tired but you have things to do:

- go to bed anyway, but set the alarm to give yourself time in the morning to do whatever you absolutely must accomplish
- teach the children to do more of their own evening preparations for school
- do more during the day in anticipation of the tired feeling you get later
- get up later and you can then go to bed later – after a week or two it will seem routine
- plan to have a leisurely sleep-in one day a week

Getting up in the morning:

- Set the alarm clock, giving yourself plenty of time to get ready and dressed. Do get dressed right away, even if that isn't your usual routine. A dressed person is more alert and ready to take on the world.
- Plan something for the morning if you don't have a job to go to. Windowshop, go to an art gallery or visit a fresh fruit and vegetable stand. Watch children's sports in the park or playground. Listen to the news and observe the weather. Plan to attend some special event in town – the opening of the new centre, a parade or dedication ceremony. Watch the start of the annual marathon race or attend the fair for an hour or two.

In the early days of your grief, allot short periods to your activities.

Managing the household

Maintaining the house/apartment

At first, do the things you like to do and put off the things you don't like doing or that don't matter, or get someone else to do them for you.

- Rearrange some of the furniture.
- Put some furniture in the basement or storage.
- Buy a new piece of furniture that delights you or that you find particularly useful.
- Store some ornaments – you can always bring them out again.
- Display some of your favorite things in obvious places so you can enjoy them.
- Carry on with routine tasks around the house, no matter whose responsibility they usually were. Go ahead and take down the storm windows, or dig up the peonies, hill the potatoes, take the drapes to the cleaners, have the eaves and flues cleaned.
- Leave painting or redecorating until you know what your financial situation is.

Housework

- Invite a "likes-to-do-housework" friend for lunch to help.
- Don't worry about it.
- Just tidy up at first.
- Do only what must be done.

- Set yourself 15 minutes or half an hour for a specific task, like laundry or windows. Then, later on, set another 20 minutes on the timer to do more or to finish the task.
- Hire help several times. True, it costs money, but perhaps keeping the house in order is more important than how much it costs when you need to save your energy.
- Let friends help at first. They will do the dishes, vacuum, dust and mop. They can be your transportation, fix squeaky door hinges, answer the phone and take messages. They won't go into your cupboards, drawers or private belongings unless you ask them to.
- Begin by just doing something. Often, you find once you've started that it is not as unpleasant or difficult as you expected.
- Do nothing for a few days. So things get dirty and the house gets messy! Then set yourself a day – next Tuesday, for instance – as the day you'll begin to get back into your housework routine.
- Take out the garbage! It must be done regardless, even though your spouse may have always done it.
- If you have large items to dispose of, call a refuse collector to haul it away. They usually charge by the square yard. The classified section of your local newspaper usually lists several people in your area who do this work. Your city may also provide a refuse removal service – phone them.

Garden and yard work

The garden and its maintenance can be a worry when you are newly widowed. Even if you have been used to doing the work of planting, weeding and other maintenance jobs, you may feel too exhausted to tackle even the smallest task. You may say "What's the use? There's no one to share it with." However, it is quite possible that contact with the earth and nature will help. Many people feel comforted when spending time in their gardens and caring for balcony planters and patio boxes. Routine is helpful for a feeling of security, and pushing yourself a little to get outside on a beautiful day could prove to be a beginning for you.

- If you have always done garden work, continue it.
- Hire people to do the necessary clean-up in the spring and fall unless you enjoy that aspect.
- If it's springtime and you aren't ready to be involved, don't bother with bedding plants. Simply maintain the shrubs and lawn.

Repairs and alterations

Learn to arrange for these yourself, rather than depending on friends.

- Write down names and phone numbers of service companies you hear about.
- Talk to friends and neighbors and find out who they call to do work.
- Phone a consumer organization or your library for information. Some newspapers have columns giving consumer advice.
- Some stores service the appliances they sell or make arrangements for repair, including pick-up and delivery.

Call repair people yourself – don't rely on a friend to call for you. You may not know what needs to be done but you can describe the problem accurately. Dial and say, "My name is _____. My (fridge, stove, garage door, dryer) doesn't work. When can you come and look at it?" Or, for a small appliance, "When are you open so I can bring it to your shop?"

Women may not be used to dealing with mechanical and motorized equipment repairs. While there are fewer female mechanics, most men do not repair their own cars either – they take them to a garage or body shop. Some men may seem more technically accurate in describing what is wrong or what they would like looked at, and more confident in requesting an estimate, but there is no reason why more women shouldn't have these basic skills also. Choose a garage as you would any repair facility – organizations, friends and co-workers for recommendations, and then request an estimate before authorizing any work. Get estimates from several shops before making your decision. Some widows take a mechanics course especially for women.

Don't get into the habit of relying on friends, relatives and neighbors to fix items or do housework for free. Continually asking for services you can buy or arrange for yourself will eventually cause hard feelings. People will hesitate to visit or call for fear that you will either hint or ask for help with another household project. Friends are happy to help occasionally, but usually come to resent being expected to provide time-consuming assistance again and again.

Sometimes you have this problem in reverse. A friend offers to help, but you don't want this person to for one reason or another – this person can't do a professional job or takes too long to fulfill the promised task.

The situation can get awkward. You wonder how you can ask someone else to repair the fence when Joe has already offered. You don't want to hurt Joe's feelings; yet he's not doing it and a month has gone by. If you can possibly hire someone else, do so, or you will end up being quite frustrated by the situation. You could then approach Joe and say, "I realized it was an imposition to ask you to repair the fence, so I have hired someone. And I want to thank you for your offer."

Your spouse's car

- Sell it.
- Use it, perhaps changing the seat covers or repainting it.
- You may feel better selling it and buying another for yourself.
- One of your adult children may want his father's or mother's car. If you can afford to give it away, you might consider this. If not, find out the value and sell it to your son or daughter. Have a written agreement to avoid misunderstanding and resentment in the future.

Sympathy for others

Some widowed people feel an unrealistic and extreme sympathy for others. You may consider giving three or four times your usual amount to charity. You may even become distressed and worry over situations you can do little about, and be unduly upset by every misfortune that you read or hear about on radio and TV. You may offer to live with a sick or older relative.

This might seem logical, in that you are now on your own and the relative seems to need assistance. Indeed, your whole family may encourage this arrangement and you may agree because of your concern for the relative and because at the moment you don't like being alone. Don't make a hasty decision on such an important matter. It will take you a year or more to adjust to your own new situation and to decide what your own needs will be.

Spouse's place at the table

- Put the table against the wall.
- Sit at it yourself.
- Place the napkin holder, sugar, salt and pepper at that place.
- Rearrange the dining room furniture.
- Eat on a tray in front of the TV.

Laying a fire and chopping wood

- Don't do it for awhile.

- Buy precut kindling and wood.
- Do it yourself and be careful.

The special chair

- Reupholster it.
- Sit in it.
- Sell it.
- Give it away.
- Move it to another room or corner of the room.

Transportation

- Get on a city bus and go as far as it goes; then return on it or by a different route. This is a good way to get to know or rediscover your city. Ask the bus company for route maps and schedules.
- Learn to drive (later on, perhaps – not right after the funeral).
- Buy a car.
- Drive your spouse's car.
- Take driving lessons or a refresher course (private lessons can be costly but might be better than joining a group in the first year of widowhood.)
- Drive to friendly, comfortable places at first.
- Ask a friend to accompany you in the beginning.
- Call taxis yourself rather than asking someone to do it for you – it is no different from ordering a pizza or a cup of coffee. Try various companies for the first few times to find out which come most quickly, have pleasant drivers and get you places on time.
- Accept rides from friends and acquaintances, but don't abuse their generosity. As soon as you can, develop your own means of transportation.

Talking business

When talking with business people and professionals:

- Do not look sad and mopey. Fake composure.
- Make a list before you talk with them, outlining what you want to cover in that discussion. Use one or two words for each thought or question to remind yourself about the impor-

tant points. For example, you might write:

car
  – lights
  – acceleration
  – tune-up

This reminds you to ask the mechanic at your local garage to check the high beams, which don't seem to be working, and to tell him that the car makes a grinding, straining noise when you accelerate. Also, you want to know how much a tune-up costs and when he can do it.

- Make appointments when possible, but if necessary, take a chance that the businessperson might be free at the time you drop in – it's worth a try.

- A phone call can often solve the problem without the need for an office or store visit.

- If you cry or show other emotions, don't apologize. Simply explain that you are going through a difficult time – "I'll be okay in a moment."

Personal grooming

Let other tasks slide, if necessary, but make an effort to maintain a neat appearance. Since you are struggling with so many new feelings and dealing with so many things, you may not pay much attention to how you look. Do not neglect yourself! You will feel better if you dress and groom yourself with care, even though it may be a chore.

Dental work

Postpone dental work depending, of course, on your dental problems, on when you had your last check-up and on what dental concerns you have. Let your dentist know you are grieving, and request short appointments if possible.

Visitors

Spending time with family and friends is something that most widows and widowers look forward to. It can be a short visit of only an hour, or longer such as a holiday weekend.

Sometimes you feel awkward sitting around and talking about the same things, and conversation gets strained. When you don't want to talk all the time and you still want to be together, consider games such as Scrabble, bridge, Trivial Pursuit, a jigsaw puzzle, or Monopoly.

People may visit without letting you know in advance. This can be an advantage because you don't have to worry about having the house tidy or refreshments ready. However, not everyone appreciates the spontaneous "dropper-inner." As your friend gets up to leave you could say "By the way, I'm getting more active these days and doing more things, so how about giving me a call before you come over next time?"

When family or friends phone to ask if they can come over and it is not convenient, discuss it until you find a suitable time.

Evenings and weekends

- Go to a play or movie once a month.
- Eat dinner out once a week, with or without company.
- Take a short class once a week for six or eight weeks.
- Play or learn to play golf.
- Plan your leisure sports for evenings or weekends – tennis, badminton, bowling, ping-pong, billiards.
- Visit a friend.
- Invite a friend over for coffee and dessert (buy the dessert unless you enjoy cooking).
- Plan activities for two or three evenings a week, e.g. shopping, crafts course, discussion club meeting.

- Check the TV schedule at the beginning of each week for interesting shows, and plan to watch those you select.
- Swim at the community pool once a week.
- Plan weekend activities ahead of time.
- Play bridge, crib or other games.

Don't feel obligated to go to all the meetings you have usually attended. Take care of yourself in the first few months of your bereavement by letting people know that you will not be attending for a while, or that you will come when you feel able.

Later on, discontinue the things you are no longer interested in.

Be selective and conserve your energy for particular interests, especially if you are employed. Think carefully before volunteering for extra tasks at this time.

Later still, look around for a new and exciting project to be involved in. Be with people you enjoy.

Religious services

- Go to church services, if you usually attend, even though you may cry or feel upset.
- Go when you feel you can, knowing that if you sit at the back, you can leave early if you want to.
- Tell the minister when you will attend.
- Ask a close friend or family member to sit with you.
- Sit in a different seat than you used to.
- Ask the minister not to point you out or comment unnecessarily if this might help you feel more comfortable. Or ask the minister to thank the congregation for their sympathy and support on your behalf and mention that you are at the service this morning.
- Go early and chat with your friends, enjoying their friendliness and concern for you.

Self-help groups

The most important thing a self-help group does is give widows and widowers a sense that they are not alone in their misery. They are relieved to realize that what they are experiencing is normal and that they will survive. They like to be with people who understand how they feel and who know the problems associated with the death of a spouse.

Not all widows and widowers want to be with others who are

grieving. Some need more privacy and may seek individual counselling.

See Appendix G for more information on support groups.

Radio listening and musical appreciation

There are so many forms of entertainment that it is possible to be kept from boredom all day without using our inner resources very much. But it is also true that some radio programs show us other people's points of view and give us the news of the day around the world.

Radio provides access to a variety of programs, from talk shows to plays and music. The local newspaper usually has program listings and highlights, so you can select the program you want to hear.

You may find that some music reminds you of happier times that you would rather not think about. This can be painful at first. Later on, you will be able to enjoy your favorite songs – a good sign that you are adjusting.

Clubs and the community centre

Hobby and interest clubs allow you to meet with those who share your enjoyment of an activity, be it bird watching, stamp collecting, bowling, ecology, art, drama, singing, bridge, or square dancing, to name just a few. Many are listed in the phone book under "Clubs."

Community centres also offer information on clubs, as well as exercise programs, sports and drop-in centres, lounge facilities, snacks, and an opportunity to meet people or visit friends. Centres also offer courses and how-to programs, from gazing at stars to planting begonia corms and learning to use your new camera.

Television-watching

Most widowed people find TV watching a good way to keep in touch with what's happening at home and in the world, as well as to relax and be entertained. Often some item on TV will form an interesting topic of discussion among friends and family.

Some house-bound people have maintained their interest in current affairs, sports, music, plays and current books by watching TV. Of course, it is necessary to establish other ways of enjoying yourself, too, but often, when you are by yourself, watching TV can be a pleasant way to spend part of your time. Choose your programs and watch with interest. It could be fun.

8

Family and Relatives

When there are young children

Talk about the dead person with the children. Don't avoid the subject – make a point of reminiscing.

A child could misinterpret you if you say the parent is sleeping or away, so use "death," "died," "dead." Encourage the children to read some of the excellent children's books on grief, or read to them.

Talk about your own feelings of grief, as much as the children can understand. This may help them to talk about their feelings too. Don't stop and leave the room every time you begin to cry. Pause to gain control of yourself, and continue to talk and answer questions. Your crying will stop after a while and the children will be reassured. Tell them that you are all right and that you won't always feel this sad.

Your children may want to talk about their mother or father at inconvenient times, but take the time to listen.

Discuss what will be different now in the way you live and the things that will remain unchanged – for instance, holidays, vacations, daily routine. Reassure them that you are still a family.

Show your children that you can be independent and capable. Depending solely on them for companionship, entertainment and even security is not wise for any of you.

If a child does not talk with you about his or her grief and concerns, arrange an opportunity for him or her to talk with a favorite relative, friend or counsellor. Perhaps your son or daughter is not expressing grief. It is also difficult when they express their grief through upsetting behaviors which often occur at inconvenient times, like before you go to work in the morning.

What do they feel? What do they need? It's hard to determine. Do they feel responsible? Small children often think that in some way they caused the death. Children may feel burdened with adult responsibility; people sometimes say to a child, "Now you are the man of the family," and he tries so hard to take the place of his father – an unsuitable role for a child of any age. Let your son or daughter know you do not expect them to take their father's or mother's place in the family with all its responsibilities and duties. They have their own special place in the family.

When talking with minor children about a parent's death, speak simply and directly for short periods of thirty seconds to ten minutes.

Realize that your child's behavior may be affected. A usually cooperative child may rebel or become stubborn, a quiet child noisy. An A-student's grades may drop, or an outgoing teenager may become quiet and withdrawn.

The child may feel guilty about something he said or thinks she did to the dead father or mother. And sometimes the fear exists that they might lose the remaining parent as well.

One young mother said, "My kids were very unnatural in the first few weeks, but gradually became their normal, demanding, often naughty, curious, rambunctious selves. I found that hard to cope with for long periods, and then I felt guilty for yelling at them because I'd think 'Poor kiddies – they just want to get back to normal and I'm holding them in sorrow just because I am edgy and sad and my kids aren't.'"

Tell your child it is natural to feel angry at the parent for dying and leaving her. Some expressions and statements you can use are: "He didn't mean to." "She was so very sick and we did all we could." "If he'd had a choice, he'd still be here." "She loved you very much and certainly didn't want to leave you."

Adult children

Adult children living at home are greatly affected by the death of a parent. They are concerned about the remaining parent who, while grieving, seems like a different person. They may be concerned about themselves as well – what will this mean to them? Can they finish schooling, will they have enough money, will they need to look for a job, find another place to live?

As the adult son or daughter of a grieving parent, you can help by:

- Urging your parent to postpone long-term financial decisions until the estate is settled.

- Not asking for extra financial assistance, and helping your parent to resist any requests for loans from other family members – at least until he or she knows what income will be needed.

- Writing short, newsy letters frequently.
- Phoning your mother or father as often as you can. Being a good listener is especially helpful.
- Encouraging your mother or father to socialize with friends and other family, and to make new friends. Your parent is responsible for his or her own social life and happiness. However, you may want to visit more often for a few months. Do not feel obliged to visit every Sunday.

Instead of asking "How are you?" each time you phone or visit, try using one of the following phrases: "What have you been doing," "What have you heard," "What have you seen," "What have you been thinking about lately," "Who have you talked with lately?" These *what, where, who, when* and *how* questions tend to encourage conversation. Other useful questions are "And what do you think of that?" and "How did you feel about that?" Use them sparingly and you will be considered interested and considerate.

- Allowing your parent to decide when she is ready and how she wants to dispose of the spouse's clothes and possessions.
- Urging the parent to remain in his home until the financial picture is clear and he is able to decide what he wants to do, i.e., stay in the present house or move.
- Encouraging the parent to go to other social events instead of spending time only with them.

Some widowed people feel they would hurt their children's feelings if they didn't visit very regularly once a week; the children therefore do them a favor by encouraging them to build their own lives as single adults. Sometimes, however, the bereaved feel as if their children are trying to get rid of them. Encouraging them to develop other interests may cause them to feel that "you don't love me any more" or "you don't care." The particular relationship between parent and children will dictate how much of this encouragement can be given by the family and how much must be left to friends or a minister or doctor. If the parent was very dependent on the spouse or children before the death, it is difficult for the family to encourage him or her to become independent without professional help.

The surviving parent's need for more help than usual during grief is normally only a temporary thing. And people usually only "lean" for a while. Children need to know that it will not go on forever; the parent will not always feel this badly. After a while the phone won't ring so often, the children won't be asked over for dinner every night, and they won't feel they must invite Father over to dinner every Sunday.

Understanding your adult child's grief

Adult children overwhelmed by grief may not be able to lend emotional or social support. Accept your children's need to grieve in their own way. Help them grieve for their parent.

Are you considering moving in with your adult child? Or having her move in with you? Look at all the pros and cons before making a decision, waiting at least a year to make an informed choice. Even if you have a chronic illness, a very small pension and you get along well with your children, living with them may not be what you want six months or two years from now.

Talking with relatives and family

- Avoid getting into arguments about your spouse's personality or finances.

- Let them know you are not prepared to discuss any shortcomings they may have perceived in the funeral or memorial service.

- Be sure they know you will not lend or give them money, even if you think you are financially secure. At a later date, when your financial status is clear, you can decide whether or not you want to lend money to your adult children. Some widowed people have discovered it is wise to have a business-like written loan agreement.

- Consider their suggestions, but make no big decisions until you have all the facts.

- Let them know you want to talk about your husband or wife. If the relative is reluctant to listen and says, "Jack, I don't want to talk about it any more – we've been over and over that before," you might reply, "I know, but I feel better talking about it as well as thinking about it, which I do when you aren't here. Could you just listen, even if you don't want to say anything?"

Here are a few more ways to initiate conversation with your adult children, parents, relatives:

"I need to talk about your mom/dad/grandmother sometimes and I notice that you change the subject when I do."

"I would like to share some memories with you that I can't talk about with anyone else."

"Please tell me what you are thinking and feeling about Mom/Dad's dying. I feel like we aren't saying what we want to. It's okay if it makes us sad. It will help us both, I think."

And to a child – "I would like to talk about Dad/Mom/Grandfather, but you look so sad when I do. Is it okay if I tell you how I feel about his/her death and what I miss? I think it would bring us closer together if we could share our grief."

You will soon know which friends and family will let you talk about the past and about your present feelings. Some people will be uneasy when you talk about your loss.

If you need to talk, phone a friend you know will listen and always ask whether the time is convenient. "I need to talk – have you time to listen?" "Is this a convenient time to talk?" or "Can you call me back when you have time to talk?"

The family and your spouse's belongings

You will likely be criticized whatever you do with your husband's or wife's personal effects. Do what you think best. Certainly you can dispose of ordinary clothing, from socks and underwear to sweaters and coats, but you may want to place items such as jewellery, awards, books, a collection or fishing gear in a safety deposit box, your basement or a commercial locker. Store them for a year or more until you decide whether to keep them (for yourself or for the children), to give them to a brother or sister or parent, or to sell them.

Your spouse's specialty tools or equipment may be especially hard for you to dispose of if he or she valued them. You may wish to keep those you can use yourself (hammer, saw, screwdriver, typewriter, sewing kit) and sell the rest. Do not try to decide during the first months after your spouse's death. When in doubt, the rule is *keep them for a while*. Then, if they have monetary value and you need the money, sell. If they have mostly sentimental value and you have the room, store them. You can always change your mind.

It is not a good idea to store your spouse's effects with a friend or relative. If you do, take a written inventory of what is stored. Give them a copy and put yours in your own safety deposit box. The reason for this is that when an article is hanging about for a long time – a familiar box or equipment, or especially furniture and tools – it sometimes begins to seem as if it belongs. It is yours, but the relative thinks it is his or hers. An inventory in writing prevents this kind of misunderstanding.

9

Holidays and Vacations

These occasions are especially trying for the widowed person. Think carefully about the best way to enjoy them. Some suggestions:

Holidays (Christmas, Thanksgiving, Easter)

- Decide that sometime in the next two or three years you will organize the holiday dinner festivities and have everyone at your place.
- Go to a resort by yourself or with a friend.
- Go on a tour alone or with a friend.
- Between social and rushed activities, set aside an hour and a half to three hours to be completely alone to think, relax or plan and to rearrange your schedule to make it a pleasant holiday.
- Do nothing special – be a free spirit for a few hours or two or three days.
- Visit relatives.
- Invite relatives and family to your place.
- Celebrate some of the holiday at your place.
- Ignore it and continue as if it were an ordinary day, knowing full well that this is what you are doing and that you won't always want to do it this way.
- Volunteer to help serve meals at the local mission, or accompany your church/association when they visit hospitals and nursing homes.

Vacations

Going on a trip in the early months after your spouse has died is not usually a good idea because you will probably do one of two things – feel so sad that you can't enjoy it, or put your grief on "hold" and have a letdown when you come home.

When you do decide to travel, begin with a short trip – two or three days at first. Gradually build up the time you spend travelling for recreation. At first, being at home and around family, friends and familiar surroundings seems to throw a net of protection around the widowed person. For your first few short vacations, you may wish to:

- Stay home and catch up on things – plan a leisurely time doing it.
- Invite a friend to visit you for a stay-at-home vacation.
- Visit relatives for a weekend.
- Visit out-of-town friends for a few days. Asking a friend to look after the house or apartment, mind the dog or garden and collect mail while you are gone, will make it easier to go away for short breaks.

Suggestions for the beginning traveller

- Talk to a travel agent. Shop around for one as you would for a doctor or an accountant. Begin your information-gathering project by seeing a travel agent who has been in business for five years or more. Ask for brochures about short excursions and the travel opportunities in your favorite "always-wanted-to-visit" state, province, city or country.
- Buy a map of the town and province or state you plan to visit. Look at the highways and rail routes; choose local sights that would be interesting to visit.
- Take short bus journeys in your part of the province or state. Leave in the morning, have lunch at your destination and return after walking around for half an hour or so in that other town or village. Once in a while, invite a friend to join you on these adventures. One of the advantages of going alone is that you usually meet more people and talk to them.
- Drive short distances from home at first, getting into more and more unfamiliar territory later in your bereavement. This way you can always return home in a few hours if you begin to feel anxious.
- Plan to arrive at any new destination early so you have a chance to look around and get your bearings.
- Join a package tour. Take day tours to begin with; then join a three or five-day tour. Tours are available by bus, plane or

ship. Talk to a travel agent for advice and suggestions.

- Buy or order a ticket – if it is an open one it is good for many months and sometimes a year. Go away for a few days.
- Read the travel sections of newspapers and magazines – many of the writers travel alone.

Staying at a hotel or resort

- Look at many brochures and ask friends and acquaintances about their experiences in choosing a resort.
- Go with a friend the first time if you are not used to travelling alone.
- Plan many activities to fill your stay. If you don't have enough time or change your mind, you can always cancel one or two.
- Ask a travel agent to make your reservation and give you an itinerary.
- Talk to the staff the first day you arrive. This way they remember you and take an interest in you, or at least know who you are.
- Talk to the other guests right at the start of your stay. "I see you like to swim. Is the pool warm?" to a guest waiting with you for the elevator and dressed in swimming attire. Or, "I haven't tried the dining room yet – do you know if they have a specialty I should try?"
- Eat in the main dining room the first night. Relax, enjoy and charge it to your room (yes, it is usually more expensive than the little coffee shop down the street).
- Go on day tours and to a dinner theater; learn to play golf; take tennis lessons.
- Buy postcards and write notes to friends while tanning on the beach or in the evening.
- Tip for good service.
- Keep a journal, notebook or photo story of what you see and do on your holiday.

Part Three
Special Cases

10
Accidental Death

Here, we present an interview with Barbara, whose husband Mike was killed in a car accident eight years ago.

While driving on a vacation in central Canada, the couple was hit by a carelessly driven car. Mike was killed, while Barbara was so badly injured (head, face and chest) that her survival was in doubt.

A resident of British Columbia, Barbara spent a month in hospital in Ottawa, Ontario, until she had recovered sufficiently to return home to Vancouver.

At the time of the accident, Barbara and Mike's two children were young adults: the son newly married, with a new job and a new home, the daughter single and living on her own.

Elsie Palmer: How did your injuries affect your grief experience?

Barbara: At first, you don't know how you feel. I didn't want to live. I thought, what's the point? My whole life was built around my husband, although I had outside interests too. When I looked at my face in the mirror, I decided I was extremely grotesque. I considered jumping through the hospital window but decided that was stupid. My poor children had gone through so much and supported me so well that it would have been cruel to do that.

So I decided that I must concentrate on getting well first. I must admit that for a while, I had to try and put Mike's death out of my mind.

I had tried to get myself to realize that he was gone, that he wasn't coming back, but it was impossible to get that feeling. Then, I thought, "Okay, let's go with that, and fantasize that he isn't really gone, that he's just away and will be coming back." That helped me until I was well enough to actually realize that he was gone.

Elsie: Do you remember the accident?

Barbara: No, and part of my problem now is that I have some loss of memory from the injuries. I do remember being in the ambulance. I remember someone holding my hand. Apparently there was a young man with me in the ambulance. Somehow in the back of my mind I thought it was my son holding my hand, and that was a great comfort.

Elsie: How did you learn of your husband's death?

Barbara: The doctor woke me; I think he must have called my name. He mentioned the hospital I was in, and said, "You've been in an accident." I remember saying, "How is my husband?" and he said "Oh, he's dead. There wasn't much we could do for him."

I just passed out; I didn't even answer.

Elsie: That must have been a terrible extra shock.

Barbara: It was. I feel it was a brutal way to tell me.

Elsie: How did you feel about not being able to attend the funeral?

Barbara: Badly, very badly. Yes, I missed it dreadfully. A friend of ours took over and arranged everything. It was a wonderful thing he did for me, but I had a real feeling of resentment. I felt gypped. When I came home, there weren't friends or family there. I felt I was coming home to nothing. It was an empty feeling.

Elsie: So that first month alone in Ottawa was a very difficult time for you. Did you feel deserted?

Barbara: I didn't feel deserted, but I felt I wasn't living in the world, like I was in a strange land. I was so sedated because of my injuries that I sort of floated from one thing to the next. I felt very, very bad. I hurt all over.

My son came and stayed with me for a while, but he was newly married with a new job and had to get back. The letters from home were a tremendous help. My daughter wrote regularly; she didn't always have much to say, but just knowing there was something in that envelope helped a lot.

One day my roommate had a cardiac arrest. I found that very difficult. I had to roll over on those broken ribs – they don't tape you, you know – to call the nurse, and I broke down and cried.

It wasn't until the end of my stay there that I began to make some decisions. And of course they were rather ridiculous. One, I decided I'd have to get married again, and two, I decided I'd have to go back to work. I'm not married, but I did return to work. I thought that if I went back to work I could prove to myself that I was capable, and it would give me something to do. I knew it would be impossible to stay around the house.

Elsie: So after a month you came back home?

Barbara: I was grieving and wasn't getting well, so they suggested that I come back home but stay in bed.

I was in bed for a month or more, getting well enough to have surgery. They also had to rebreak my jaw because it had set wrongly in the meantime.

My daughter came to live with me and that was a tremendous help because I couldn't do anything. I was home for about six months before I could take care of myself again.

Elsie: During that six months, were you feeling the real impact of your grief?

Barbara: Yes. One of the worst things was the desperation. My husband was quite often home for lunch, and it was the worst feeling to know that he'd never be there again.

Occasionally I started crying and simply couldn't stop. It was so devastating that I suppose you would say I was physically impaired. I remember once crying so hard in the basement that I could hardly climb the stairs. It completely saps your strength.

Then there was this terrible ache in my arms, because I am an affectionate person and I just ached to put my arms around him. I must say I hugged the devil out of the dog and cat.

I'd try to make a mental note of how I felt, and I realized that about every two weeks I felt just a bit better. This was a real challenge, or goal. I thought, "Gee, if I feel this much better today, how will I feel in two weeks' time?" Oh, I had my bad days, my terrible days, but I'd think to myself, "This isn't going to last forever. Remember the last time you felt this low, you came back again."

And I did get dressed and get out of the house often. I breathed the fresh air and became acutely aware of things I hadn't been aware of before – flowers, birds, the beauty and shape of a tree, the sky. To me, dark clouds had always meant rain. Now I started looking at them from a different viewpoint. They were interesting; they would change and disappear.

Elsie: So you became more acutely aware of life.

Barbara: Very much so. I realized – I suppose it's what every mother goes through – I felt that now was the time to make sure the children realized how deeply I love them and how much they mean to me. I thanked them and said I just couldn't have gotten along without their help.

Elsie: Did you have any trouble sleeping?

Barbara: At first I had nightmares, but I think that was because of the drugs. I was on morphine every four hours for about five days.

Then after I was home I had a great deal of trouble sleeping. It was the hollowness, the emptiness. I'd just lie awake for hours. They gave me sleeping pills. The cure was worse than the problem sometimes. I'd be sleepy until early afternoon and wide awake in the evening. I was also taking pills for depression then.

Then I decided it was ridiculous to carry on that way, that I had better get with it. So I stopped taking the pills. I still have the bottle. I don't need them; I am stronger. But I keep it to remind me how far I have come. Mind you, after I got rid of the pills, a wee glass of sherry helped relax me after I crawled into bed!

I would also write down my thoughts when it got really bad. I liked sketching how I felt. I remember once drawing ribs, human ribs. I felt I was sewn inside a skeleton.

I like to write poetry – ridiculous things. They rhymed but they didn't necessarily make sense. I found that if I put things on paper I got them out of my mind.

Elsie: Writing things out is a very useful tool. It's marvellous that you discovered it.

Barbara: Well, I had always written a little poetry – just for my husband, not anyone else. I couldn't write deep things because I wasn't that type – just humor. One day I was thinking about things and I thought, "I'll just put it down on paper." I've saved them, and periodically I look back at them. That's when I realize how much better I am now. You've got to praise yourself a little bit.

Elsie: I think you have to praise yourself a lot! So, you felt you were making progress even though you were still not well. Can you pinpoint a time when you thought there was a turning point?

Barbara: One thing that really bothered me was my husband's belongings, and I finally sent his clothes away. I wish now I'd had some help. I was offered help, but I thought I should be able to do it myself.

Over the years we had all given clothes to Central City Mission and my husband felt strongly that was where things should go. So that's where I sent his clothes. I remember a volunteer man came up to get them and all he had was a little Volkswagen and these clothes were in a box on top of the roof rack. But I felt my husband was behind me and I had done the right thing.

The other turning point was a year later, when I decided what to do with his ashes, and had the strength to do it. Mike was always a free spirit, so I threw his ashes off the Lions Gate Bridge.

Elsie: During the year that followed the accident, did you have to appear in court?

Barbara: No, I was in and out of the hospital that whole year. When their insurance adjustors and legal counsel finally came to Vancouver to interview me, I had to meet them at the board room in the insurance office downtown. It was exactly a week after one of my operations and

I wasn't very strong.

I had to sit at a table with about twelve different people and be cross-examined. And I had to decide how to answer. I remembered my husband commenting once when talking about an investigation he was on, saying, "Don't hurry for an answer; take your time."

One question was what I ate for lunch that day. I remembered very well, because I had made a pig of myself and eaten two chicken pies. And they said, "And what did you have to drink – tea, coffee and maybe a bottle of beer?" And I thought, "Trying to trick me, you devil." But my lawyer told me afterwards I did very well.

They also tried to say I was driving the car. I do have some loss of memory from the accident, but I wasn't driving.

Elsie: Did going to that meeting set you back?

Barbara: No. If anything, it made me mad, and I hadn't been able to feel mad for a year. I was annoyed at them. But I was pleased with myself for how I handled them.

I had thought it would be cut and dried because the other person was clearly responsible. But I had to go over it all and they asked so many things that did not seem pertinent at all. Where I was born, my relationship with my husband, my relationship with the kids and my in-laws, where I was educated, what I had done – everything in my life! I have a stack of papers about three inches high of questions I had to answer and forms I had to fill in.

Elsie: How long were you kept in the past because the court case wasn't settled?

Barbara: It was finally settled out of court, but that wasn't for four years.

During that time I went back to work for a year and a half because I wouldn't give in, but I was still having terrible health problems. I had to have so many operations, and my sight was impaired – I had double vision – and I couldn't gain weight.

My opthalmologist said, "You will never be right until you have this court case settled." I thought he was giving me the runaround, although I really liked him. But he was right. After the case was settled I was able to eat properly again and stopped having diarrhea, and my eyesight improved.

I'm sure it was the long letter I wrote to my lawyer telling him how bad I felt because things were dragging on so long. I think that helped to set the ball rolling. The case was settled shortly after that.

Elsie: Do you have any anger over the fact that your husband was killed by a careless driver?

Barbara: No.

Elsie: That his life was cut short?

Barbara: I'm sad about that part, but my husband did live a very full life. He was glad to see his family grown. In fact, he mentioned on the trip that he was very pleased our son had married such a nice girl. Also, we had met my future son-in-law at that time and we were really very happy.

As for the driver of the other car, no, I bear no animosity whatever. It was an accident. It wasn't premeditated. I'm sure his family felt badly. It must have been a terrible strain on them. It was carelessness, but it was an accident.

Elsie: You mentioned that writing and sketching helped you to get through your grief. Was anything else especially helpful?

Barbara: I found music helpful, too. For a while I wasn't brave enough to play the songs I liked, but later I could go back and remember the really, really happy part of my life.

Sometimes I wonder if they shouldn't change the marriage vows. I was re-reading a letter from our minister about how in marriage your lives are entwined; you become one. That is lovely, and I felt that way about our marriage. But I think a person should keep part of their life to themselves, to be independent. The fact that I had worked before and had been fairly independent made adjusting easier.

I suppose I must say I was my own best friend, too. I did cater to myself after Mike died. I thought how all those years we had denied ourselves certain things, saving for a rainy day. But there couldn't have been a rainier day on top of my tears. So, I thought, "Now's the time to enjoy it."

After I had been a widow for about a year, I joined a support group. That was very, very helpful. It meant I was with people who knew exactly how I felt. If I broke down while I was talking, nobody scolded or felt embarrassed. Everybody encouraged you to talk.

In those days I was lonely and probably apt to talk too much. It was hard to shut the old voice off. But everybody understood that. Your friends think they can help you, but some don't have the understanding and they don't have the time.

Elsie: Do you feel you have adjusted from your grief?

Barbara: Oh yes. I still have my down days, but I think that's mostly because of the injuries. I'll never be one hundred percent the way I was before the accident. I had some brain damage, and don't learn some things as easily as I would like. I find if I take everything at a slower speed, I can do just about everything I want to do.

Elsie: What are the most important things for you right now?

Barbara: I'm fortunate to have grandchildren. They mean a lot to me and I know I mean a lot to them. Also, I volunteer one day a week at the Red Cross and get a great deal of satisfaction out of that. It is very worthwhile and they are a great group of people. And I recently started to travel a little and find it very rewarding.

I enjoy living every day. I read an article that said, "The ending is a beginning." And it really is. I don't think I could be doing much better.

An interview with Sandra, mother of three, whose husband was murdered by a burglar five years ago. Their youngest child was a small baby and the others were preschoolers. Sandra was in her late twenties and Steve in his thirties when he died.

Elsie Palmer: Tell me a little about how your husband died.

Sandra: An acquaintance of ours broke into the house in the middle of the night and came down the hall toward the bedroom where we were sleeping. The cat's meowing woke me up. I woke Steve and told him the cat was in. He went out into the hall and I heard him say, "Oh, my God." Then someone came running, screaming into the bedroom with my husband after him.

This fellow fell on top of me and Steve fell on him. When I pushed the man off me, I recognized him. I told Steve who it was and he said, "He's got me," and collapsed.

I didn't know it then, but Jerry, this acquaintance, had stabbed my husband, and Steve had managed to pull the knife out of his back and stab Jerry in the arm.

Jerry said, "I'm sorry, I'm sorry, I was so afraid." By this time, Steve was yelling at me to get an ambulance, so I called one.

When I went back to him, he was out of the bedroom and lying on the hall floor dying.

Elsie: You knew he was dying?

Sandra: I knew he was dying and he had the knife in his hand. It was the first time I had seen the knife.

Elsie: Did your children wake up?

Sandra: Yes, the baby was screaming. Then the ambulance men came. I ran upstairs to phone my neighbor, and while I was phoning my eldest daughter came out of her room. The neighbor came and took the children to her home. The police came, and a neighbor went with Steve to the hospital while I stayed and talked with the police.

Elsie: Were you feeling anything at this time?

Sandra: Just fear. I was very dry-mouthed and wanted a cup of coffee desperately. I got up to make myself a cup of coffee. I guess I was in shock.

Later on, the neighbor came back and told me Steve had died. So more police came, and I was taken across to a neighbor's house where they did the interview for the police records.

Elsie: Did you find answering their questions very difficult, or were you still too much in shock?

Sandra: Everybody else found it extremely difficult. I didn't at all. I wanted to tell them what happened. The neighbors said, "Oh, does she have to go through this right now?" and "How much more do you want? Surely that's enough?"

Elsie: Do you think you were so numb that you didn't feel anything? Or was it just a relief to say what happened?

Sandra: I think it was both. It was like I was relating a story, and that's how it was for weeks.

Elsie: Without any feelings?

Sandra: Yes. If I related it, it was with no feelings because I only talked about it when I had complete control.

Elsie: Never when you were upset?

Sandra: Not at the beginning. Of course, nobody asked me either. I guess they didn't want to remind me.

Elsie: So, then did you tell the children about it?

Sandra: No, they put me to bed, which I realize was the worst thing. I had brandy and tranquillizers and they put me to bed, but the phone was ringing constantly. It was very loud and grated on my nerves terribly.

Elsie: They were answering the phone?

Sandra: Yes. I was supposed to be sleeping. Of course, I wasn't, but then I was worried. I had tried to get through to my husband's parents, who lived overseas, and I was very worried about them – how they were going to take it and what I was going to say.

Finally, I did get through to them and they took it extremely well. They were in shock, I guess. His mother couldn't believe it.

My own parents were away. They were also going through a crisis, as Mum was having an operation on her shoulder. I called Dad at the hotel, thinking Mum was still in the hospital. Well, it happened that she had come out that morning and was there when I called.

Steve had just had a serious operation three months before and we thought he might die, so when I said Steve was dead, my father asked, "How did he die?" I told him and he said, "Oh. He's been murdered." That was the worst moment because my mind rebelled against that word. My mother went hysterical in the background and I told him to call me back after he had calmed her down. That was the worst up to that point.

I don't know why, but I didn't want to see the children. I didn't think I was postponing it. I didn't want to have to tell them and I guess I just couldn't cope with any more at that time. However, when my oldest daughter asked after her dad, the neighbors thought I had better come, so they came and got me.

The children were playing in the back garden and I told them out there.

Elsie: How did you tell them? Do you remember?

Sandra: Yes, I sat down and had them standing before me and I said that Daddy had died. A neighbor was cradling the middle one, who was crying, and I had the eldest one, but she wasn't crying. She just put up with my cuddling and said, "I want to go and watch the boy on the skateboard."

It's funny – twice in the last two weeks, she has been crying about her daddy. That's the first time I have seen her cry about it. She said, "When you told us, I didn't want to believe it. I couldn't believe it." It has taken five years.

The first time, she came to me at night. She said she couldn't sleep, she missed her daddy. I said, "I've been waiting for this – why now?" And she said, "I can't take the hurt any longer."

Now, Michele, the middle one, she could always cry. The oldest one said to me, "Doesn't Michele miss Daddy?" You see, I had forgotten to tell her who has cried over the years. I've cried, the baby has cried, Michele has cried, but not the oldest.

Michele probably doesn't miss her daddy right now.

Elsie: Maybe she has resolved her grief.

Sandra: Also, she's not pre-adolescent, and all those emotions you don't understand aren't happening yet. But she has adapted better. The oldest one remembers more and was much closer to her father.

Elsie: I remember you saying the little one was missing having a father.

Sandra: Yes, she really wants a dad. She was just saying the other day,

"When are you going to get married again?"

That's another thing that was bothering the oldest one. Was I going to get married? She was worried about that. We are a cohesive unit now, and I can see her thinking that a stranger will come in. They would have to accommodate him and it would upset the applecart.

So I reassured her about replacing her dad. She said, "Do I have to call him Dad?" and I said no, she didn't.

She wanted to know if she would be adopted and her name changed, and I said not unless she wanted to. So, all these things have been bothering her. "I don't know anybody now," I said, and I told her not to worry about it. I said I'd tell her when to worry. "And for heaven's sake, don't worry on the first and second date." So we end up smiling.

She says it hurt too much before, but it's beginning to hurt less now, so she can talk about it.

Elsie: Her wanting to go away and play didn't mean she didn't care; it was just all she could think of to get away from what was happening.

Sandra: Oh, I knew that. And the following day, the house was so full of people and relatives that I sent her to school. I guess she spent half the morning in the bathroom and she remembers that.

Elsie: So then what happened? People started to arrive for the funeral?

Sandra: Yes, and his parents. I was anxious about that but they were fine.

I think I thought everything was going along fine, but it wasn't. I was being well insulated from everything and I guess I was insulating myself. I remember that I wanted to talk to the mother of the person who killed my husband and they told me I couldn't. It upset me terribly at the time.

Elsie: What did you want to say to her?

Sandra: I was concerned about how everybody else was feeling and this went on for a long, long time. I felt so terrible for Jerry's parents. Looking back now, I guess my anger was so deep that I couldn't even recognize it and expressed it the other way around, as concern. My behavior wasn't really appropriate that first year.

But anyway, everybody came to the funeral and I decided not to have a coffin at the church. There had been several deaths very recently and every time, Steve had said, "Oh, no, not another coffin." I knew it bothered him to have the coffin there.

Also, I didn't think I could take it and didn't know how his parents would take it. But that was an error, because after the funeral they wanted to see him and, of course, I hadn't arranged for that at all. He wasn't prepared for anyone to see him.

Elsie: What did you do?

Sandra: I just said, "No, you can't. Please don't." But I can see their feelings now.

Elsie: Do you think if you had seen him the reality would have hit you more? Did you ever regret not seeing him?

Sandra: No, because I once saw an aunt in her coffin and that's how I remember her. Now I don't remember her when she was alive. Also, I believe in the spirit leaving the body so I thought, "He's with me, he's not in that body."

Elsie: It's always a controversy. Viewing the body seems so important to some people. They think you aren't dealing with your grief if that doesn't happen. Do you believe that?

Sandra: No, I don't think so. You are in shock anyway. I don't think it would matter one way or the other. After all, I saw him die. He was literally dying in my arms, so I really didn't have to see him again. I also considered what he would want. It was as though there were two people dealing with this. Every decision I made, I would think, "What would Steve want?" That went on for a good year.

Elsie: How long did you stay with the neighbors?

Sandra: Five or six days. Then I moved back into the house. No one could understand my going back. But I did, and it didn't bother me. It was a comfort to me. Even though Steve was dead, it was still home. It was familiar.

Elsie: Can you tell me, when did you really start to feel things?

Sandra: Six weeks after Steve's death we travelled to spend the summer with my parents. On the way, I had car trouble and that really threw me. After the car was patched up and we got to where we were spending the night, I put the kids to bed and took a bath myself. I was in the bath, when all of a sudden it came crashing down on me and all I could say was, "Dead. He is really dead." I had gone six weeks and it hadn't hit me till then.

That was the beginning of really grieving. Before that I had thought I was doing so well. So then I started searching for answers. I started searching for books to help me.

Elsie: What did you find most helpful?

Sandra: The two Catherine Marshall books, *To Live Again* and *Beyond Ourselves*. I couldn't believe anyone else would feel the way I did, but there it was in words. That was a beginning, to realize that what I was going through was normal.

After the summer, I had to go back home again, and that was very painful. The summer had been painful, too, but I was numb and in a daze most of the time. When I came back, that's when I really felt it. I sure needed a lot of strength to cope.

The court date would come up every month. It happened that the court date coincided with my menstrual cycle and I was feeling fragile then anyway.

Elsie: Did you have to go to court?

Sandra: No, a friend went for me, and he would report back. But nothing was going on, just one remand after another. I can't really say I felt anger then. That came later. It was just a terribly empty state.

I had a hysterical reaction about five months after we were back home. I thought I was dying. The doctors asked, "Who are you talking to about your feelings?" And of course I wasn't talking to anybody. So every week I'd go and talk to the family doctor and that helped a great deal. Still, I didn't feel anger. It would have been much better if I had.

Elsie: And you felt lonely?

Sandra: Terribly lonely. I felt lonely and lost. I'd be fine for two or three days and suddenly my whole world would collapse. Everybody would say, "Oh, she's doing so well. She's so fantastic." Somebody would come in the evening and I would be fine; they would leave and I would just break apart.

Elsie: Did you share those feelings with anyone?

Sandra: Well, a minister was coming to visit me and every time he came, it felt like peace descended on the house. He was an incredible person.

With some people I could share my feelings and with others I couldn't. I felt some people couldn't handle it. You know how people say, "How are you? and you say, "Fine," automatically? But when some people would say, "Are you really fine?" then I'd break down. I'd choose who I'd break down with.

Elsie: You could easily assess which ones really wanted to know?

Sandra: Definitely. And if they picked up how I felt and fed it back to me, that was another clue that they really wanted to know. There were only a few like that.

Elsie: Did you think there was a time period at the end of which you would feel better?

Sandra: I was hoping at the end of a year. "They" said, "time heals," and that was the worst thing you could say to me because I didn't want any time. I got very depressed and time was my enemy. I wanted it to be all over with, like it never happened. I wanted some joy again.

Elsie: There was none in that first year?

Sandra: Superficial, yes, sure; but not deep down. Towards the end of the first year, I began to get this feeling of accomplishment. I began to think, "I've had a week where I have felt much better." I started reaping the benefits of all this "work." I began to have more confidence and see the children progressing.

Elsie: What would have been the most helpful things someone could have done for you at the beginning?

Sandra: Give me a hug, I think. Even now, the main thing missing in my life is someone to hug me. When a close friend says, "How are you?" with a hug, if you are fine you give them a hug back and a little chuckle and get on with your conversation. If you are not fine, that hug breaks down your barriers and it will all come flooding out. A hug from a friend says, "You can share with me."

Elsie: And a year later, what would be the best thing?

Sandra: Don't tell them that in a year or two it's going to be better. Someone told me that at the end of three years I would be married and that meant, to me, that in three years everything would be back to normal. I wanted to believe that. I was hoping it would be so. At the end of year three I wasn't married, but, of course, "they" didn't know any more than I did. So don't say, "Oh, well, you should be feeling better by now" and "you'll get married."

Elsie: Do you think it has taken you longer because your husband was murdered?

Sandra: I'm sure of it, because I'm afraid a lot now. I have to fight it constantly. I'm afraid of new situations. In the back of my mind is a nagging little voice when I go into a room, a house that's been empty, an underground garage – any place where there is the slightest danger. I don't know if it will ever go.

I had an anxiety attack in November. I didn't know what it was; I thought I was allergic to some fish I had eaten. I couldn't breathe and had to go to the hospital. Once I realized what was happening, I said, "Okay, things aren't going as well as you think they are. What's the problem?" Then I suddenly realized what it was. I had read in the newspaper that a murderer had escaped; he was from the town I was visiting at the time. That triggered an attack all these years later.

Elsie: Did you go to court for the trial?

Sandra: No, it would have been better if I had gone. I'm afraid of something I can't visualize anymore. I never saw Steve's attacker again after he left the house that morning, and I live with this.

Elsie: What else was most helpful or unhelpful after the first year had passed?

Sandra: By the end of the first year, I was beginning to resent the fact that I was a prominent man's widow. Everybody knew who he was, and I was just his widow. I began to ask, "What about me?" So I moved away to another town. That was traumatic, but it was a good thing.

The second year was not as painful as the first, but it had many painful moments because everything I avoided in the first year I hit in the second.

Elsie: Like what?

Sandra: Guilt, depression and then I found out that the depression was anger I hadn't been able to deal with.

Elsie: Did you get help with this?

Sandra: Yes, I went to a support group and I was also seeing a psychiatrist.

The psychiatrist couldn't believe that I hadn't had any sort of therapy. Because of the violence involved, it wasn't ordinary grief. It wasn't an ordinary death. Once I started going to him, everything began to make sense – the way I dealt with some things and avoided others. That second year was a year of getting to know myself.

Elsie: And accepting yourself.

Sandra: No, not the second year. Maybe the fourth year I began to accept myself.

Elsie: Were you still criticizing yourself in the second year?

Sandra: I didn't like the way I was treating the children. I wasn't happy; I was downright miserable. I may have been making some progress, but I knew I could make much more.

I felt abnormal and very guilty for still being so vulnerable. Everyone said, "After the first year, the first year. . ." Well, it took me that long to get over the emptiness and numbness and into the initial sadness and grief.

Elsie: So you would tell someone who is trying to help not to put a time limit on grief? If it takes ten years. . .

Sandra: I think I'd begin to worry after ten years; I'd think there was some difficulty. But not after one year, two years, five or six, depending on the relationship you had with your spouse.

Elsie: What bothers you most now?

Sandra: Well, the loneliness. I went to single parents but that didn't fill my needs. I'm going to school now, so I have that interest. I've decided to just let be what will be. If I meet a man I like, that's fine.

Elsie: Meeting men is not one of your priorities?

Sandra: Last year I was very upset because I hadn't met a nice man to go out with. I was lonely and became depressed over this. I didn't really do anything about it, but it bothered me. I thought, "You ought to get out there and meet men."

But now I feel that I will, but that I will meet them through my own interests. That way I will develop as a person. I can't go out with the objective of meeting a man I'll like and he'll like me. It doesn't work.

Elsie: What about sex? Is it a problem for you?

Sandra: Yes, I miss it. Sometimes if I'm getting cranky, I realize what it is.

Elsie: Acknowledging the problem is enough without doing something about it?

Sandra: Yes, I couldn't feel that my sex urge was becoming unbearable and then relieve it by picking someone up. No. Because I'd get nothing out of that. I'd feel degraded.

Elsie: You are now making plans and you do have some fun now, don't you?

Sandra: Oh yes, I'm quite happy. Now I can say I'm a happy person – with ups and downs, but still I can say I'm more at peace.

Elsie: When did you start feeling that?

Sandra: Just this year. I went on a holiday last year, and lying in the hot sun on the sand I said to myself, "Why don't you do this more often? Why don't you treat yourself better?" That's the first time I really began to feel good. Up to then, I hadn't realized that I was ignoring myself while looking after the children, the house, the dog, the cat and everybody else.

Elsie: Do anniversaries bother you?

Sandra: They used to, but not any more. The anniversary of his death bothered me for three years. The fourth year I really can't say it did. Christmas and birthdays don't bother me now either.

Elsie: When did you remove your wedding ring?

Sandra: At the end of the first year. I'd be out socially at a party and someone would say, "Where is your husband?" I'd have to say he died, and I found that difficult. Then when I started making my own decisions and seeing them through, and became a single person figuring out these problems – well, then I wasn't married any more! I was single. It was a gradual process.

Elsie: Did you find it helpful to meet with other women in the support group?

Sandra: Oh yes, but it would have helped more if I had gone in the first year. It helped because I could talk. Also, I didn't know many single people before I went to the support group – most of my friends were couples. It helped to meet people who were on the same wavelength as me.

12
Death after a Long Illness

An interview with widower Lawrence, whose wife Margaret died of a kidney disorder seven years ago after a long illness. He was in his 60s; Margaret was 62. They had two adult sons living on their own and a teenage daughter living at home when their mother died.

Elsie: Tell me how your wife died.

Lawrence: Well, she was on a kidney machine at home for five years. Even while she was on it, she pretty well looked after the running of the house and the everyday business while I worked.

But, in the latter part of her illness, she couldn't get out on her own and she had to wait till I came home and then I took her out in a wheelchair.

Elsie: How long did that go on?

Lawrence: The last eight months before her death.

Elsie: So, while you were at work, your daughter helped?

Lawrence: No, she was at school. We had a homemaker. We had had two or three that weren't too helpful, but then the last one we got was excellent. She had been a nurse and we never wanted for anything. She was always there. If I was late coming home she would stay, even though she had a family of her own.

Elsie: And your wife looked after the finances.

Lawrence: She looked after everything, even to buying my clothes. In fact, I didn't even know what size I wore. I couldn't coordinate colors.

Elsie: Well, you look good now.

Lawrence: (laughing) With a daughter like I've got, you have to.

Elsie: How old was your daughter when your wife died?

Lawrence: She was a teenager.

Elsie: That was hard for her, I guess.

Lawrence: Yes, she took it very hard. Both boys had moved out and had their own families. She was stuck at the house all the time.

Elsie: She had a lot of responsibilities then.

Lawrence: That's right. She stood up very well to it.

Elsie: And did either one of you think ahead to the fact that this was going to end and she was going to die?

Lawrence: Oh yes, when the doctor told us that her kidneys were gone. She would have up to four or five years after she went on the dialysis machine, and he was accurate to within a few months.

Elsie: Did you begin to grieve when you found out about your wife's illness?

Lawrence: No, my grieving started from the day she died. Really, I thought that there was no use worrying over something that hadn't happened yet. A very good friend who was robust, his wife was in a wheelchair (she had been for a year), he just dropped dead and she is still alive. So, the way we looked at it, I could go anytime, with the long hours I was working and working on the water. You never cross that bridge till you come to it. And we knew what we had. We spent as little time apart as possible the last year.

Elsie: How long were you married?

Lawrence: Thirty-six years. We only had one real fight in the whole time. She threatened to go back to England. I told her she could go – here's the money – but she couldn't take the kids. She didn't go, but the next year she went back for a visit.

When she wanted a new car, I got her a new car. When she wanted new furniture – well, she bought it, really, because she looked after the money.

When she died I didn't even know what banks we were dealing with. I didn't know we had to pay sewer and water tax, though I knew about the land tax. I learned everything after she died because she did it all, even when she was in a wheelchair. I went in to cash a cheque at the bank we had dealt with for twenty-five years, and they wouldn't cash it because they didn't know me.

Margaret saved all the time – this money that I have for extras. It was all saved so when we retired we could go on trips.

Elsie: What are some of the things that helped after your wife died?

Lawrence: The main things that helped, I would say, were my boss and my job. They gave me time off when Margaret was alive, when I had to put her on dialysis. Then when she died they said "Okay, we gave you that time off – now you have to make up for it." So I worked long hours every day and traveled for the job and when I got home, I really didn't have time to think.

Elsie: That helped, did it?

Lawrence: Oh, yes. The grief was there, but you couldn't feel sorry for yourself because there was too much to do. The family would come over for dinner. I like to cook. I cooked everything and they would clean up afterwards.

Elsie: How long since your wife died now?

Lawrence: Seven years.

Elsie: Would you say you have "adjusted?" Would that be a term you would use?

Lawrence: Yes, I imagine I've adjusted. I entertain and go out. I have friends, my family and I am a member of several organizations – Museum of Flight, our community centre and the Legion. There were friends and organizations that helped out too.

Elsie: Did you ever talk about your grief and how you felt?

Lawrence: Oh yes, I've never been ashamed of it. You see, we knew it was coming years before. So we made the best of what we had.

Elsie: So, in a way, you prepared for it.

Lawrence: That's right. I have no regrets, but there was only one thing that we didn't do that she wanted to do – she wanted to go to Hawaii and I didn't. We toured Europe, we toured England, we went to Expo in Montreal, we went all through the States. We had a good life. Even when she was on the machine we toured the province.

Elsie: Is there anything other people could've done for you, after she died, that they didn't do?

Lawrence: The only thing was that married friends drifted away. They would say, "Well, we'll have to have dinner together, we'll have to have suppers together." A couple of them did but after that there was – I never thought about it too much, maybe they were Margaret's friends and not mine.

And suppose you want to go out to play bridge, what are you going to do with a fifth wheel? They've got an extra one there and all the same bunch had been playing bridge. You went out to dinner and it was still the same thing. They figure, well, when you are buying drinks for three, they are only buying for one! They're embarrassed. My new friends don't feel this way.

Elsie: So now you have new friends?

Lawrence: Yes, because there are very few of the people where we've lived for twenty-five years that I have any friendship with any more. I say hello and talk to them and that's it.

Elsie: What did you do right after your wife's death that helped?

Lawrence: I worked hard and I went to lacrosse with the grandchildren, soccer games and their hockey. When I was in with those people they were very good, they accepted me. I flew east with the lacrosse team for the national finals. I went to Seattle with the hockey team. I just didn't have time to feel sorry for myself.

There were things I could do that I hadn't been able to do when Margaret was alive. It is a long grind when you can't go out to an association meeting or anything like that because you'd always worry about her at home. But when I had to be away I was in constant radio contact.

Elsie: You know that a lot of widowers marry within the first two years.

Lawrence: I've never thought of marriage. I have women friends who are partners to go to dances. I have never discussed marriage with anybody. It could change, who knows, but the way life is right now, it's about as full as I can make it. Mind you, I still miss having someone to ask, "Will I do this, will I do that?" When you invest your money, there's no one to ask, "Should I put it in here, should I put it there, what will I do with it?" You think the rugs need cleaning – you look at them and you've got nobody to ask. When you're setting the table, does the spoon go on the right or the left? But that feeling only lasts a little while.

Elsie: Would you say the way your family was before your wife died had something to do with the way they have been since?

Lawrence: Yes, the family had been awfully close. All our family had been.

Elsie: Do you cook for yourself?

Lawrence: Oh, yes. I would rather eat my own cooking than go to any restaurant.

Elsie: And you volunteer for several organizations.

Lawrence: Yes, that's what I've liked more than anything else, because many people have helped me. For instance, with the Red Cross, I used to be a blood donor all the time. I figured that when my wife needed it and my children needed it, it was there and they gave to us.

Elsie: There was a trip you took that was a turning point for you. Can you tell me about it?

Lawrence: Yes, I can still remember that trip. It was so different from anything I had ever done before, where I did what I wanted, not to please somebody else. I just started out and I did whatever turned me on. If I felt like getting up at four in the morning and going, I went.

Elsie: Do you think that your life is different from other widowers'?

Lawrence: Maybe, yes, because I have family close by and the family gets along well together.

Elsie: So what do you want to do with your life now?

Lawrence: As I'm retired, I do volunteer work and enjoy family get-togethers. Four nights a month I go to the dinner dances at the Legion since I've been on my own. I have one set of long-time friends that I still play bridge with.

Elsie: What would you say to another man whose wife has died? What advice would you give?

Lawrence: I would suggest getting out and being active in something that interests him and being with people.

Elsie: Thank you for talking with me.

Appendix A
A Summary of the Grief Process*

This is a process of adjustment – it takes time.

1. **Shock, Disbelief and Numbness** – allows the grieving person to go through the first few days without feeling very much. This period may last for a few days, a few weeks or months.

2. **Realization of Loss** – when the numbness starts to wear off, then comes the most painful period of the process. The overwhelming feelings of anguish, desolation and despair are difficult to express in words.

   Emotions – Anger, guilt, sadness, depression, loneliness, exhaustion, fear, anxiety, panic, resentment, regret, emptiness.

   Physical signs – crying and sobbing, sleeplessness (or sleeping more), loss of appetite (or eating more), irritability, hostility, inability to concentrate, absent- mindedness, restlessness.

   Need to rationalize – asking "why me?," "why him?," "why us?" Resentment expressed, sometimes anger at God, fate, minister, relatives, funeral director, medical personnel, the person who has died. Also saying, "If only I had said. . . ," "If only we had done or not done. . . ."

3. **Acceptance** – letting go of the person who died. Letting go of guilt and regrets about the past.

   Accepting the fact that life is not fair.

   An important time for the bereaved to start looking at her or his own life. Thinking of new beginnings and opportunities to build a new life.

4. **Reinvestment** – of love and energy – in other things and other relationships. Sometimes this can be an entirely new interest, or the renewal of some interest that gave satisfaction at some earlier period in the person's life.

   Note: This is not a smooth process. The grieving person will probably take two steps forward, then one back. Grief can sometimes be retriggered by an unexpected memory of the past. This can be very discouraging, and friends should remind the bereaved person that this does not mean he/she is slipping back to the first phase of grief – it is only a temporary setback.

© 1979 Elsie Palmer

For permission to copy, write to L.I.F.E. Resource Centre, #101, 395 West Broadway, Vancouver, B.C. V5Y 1A7

Appendix B
How the Spouse Died

- My wife died of cancer. Isabel had a mastectomy but the cancer had already spread.
- Kevin was so healthy. He did everything right. I can't see how he could die of a heart attack.
- My wife died of a stroke. Phyllis was in a coma for a week before she died.
- Karl had had three strokes and a heart attack and recovered from them, so I wasn't expecting him to die yet.
- Roger had emphyzema but he actually died of a heart attack.
- Ida was old like me, and she fell and broke her hip. It didn't mend properly. She never got out of bed again. There was one problem after another – bedsores, her bladder wouldn't work and then finally a virus.
- Patrick broke his neck diving into a half-filled pool. He died in front of us all.
- He died when his plane crashed. They didn't find Lucas for three years.
- My wife always had a heart problem. Not a year went by that Jessie didn't have to be rushed to the hospital in an ambulance and they'd tell us it was touch and go and we'd think for sure that this was the end. Then after a few weeks she'd be just fine and come home. This time she didn't.
- Gregg was lost at sea. A bit of his boat was picked up by fishermen but that's all.
- He went on a hiking trip. We think Keith's dead. He's been declared dead legally.
- My wife died in a house fire. Barbara was overcome by smoke.
- Joyce died in a car accident. Our car was hit by a drunk driver.
- I knew my Clifford had cancer, but I never thought he would die of it.

– My husband was shot during a robbery. In hospital Brent didn't say anything, just looked at us. He died two hours after it happened.

– Mary had an operation for a tumor and they said they couldn't get it all and that she should have radiation and chemotherapy. She spent the last year and a half of her life in hospital.

– We were in the crosswalk and Mona was hit by a car we didn't even see, it came so fast.

– Harold drove well and wasn't a drinker, but it was a rainy night and the police said there were several accidents because of bad weather conditions.

– My husband had heart trouble lately. Gordon died in his chair in front of the TV.

– Kathryn was driving home from the meeting at ten o'clock and was rear-ended by a drunk driver.

– Andre had too many drinks at the party. He drove up on a sidewalk, hit a lady (it broke her leg) and crashed into the building. He died three weeks later, mostly because of the chest injuries.

– My wife died of a cerebral hemorrhage. Carolyn was only thirty years old.

– She drowned. One minute Laura was fine, and the next we couldn't see her swimming. The doctor said that she must have got a cramp suddenly and couldn't call for help.

– It was a plane accident – an engine failed or something. That's what they said at the inquest. It was three months before they got David out, as they had to wait till spring.

– They phoned me from the golf club and said Ely died on the fourth hole. We'd been married fifteen years and he never missed a day of work. The doctor said he'd had a heart attack.

– Gerald died in a plane crash.

– I don't know what happened exactly. Ronald was hit on the head in a bar. He often went for a drink with his buddies on Friday nights after work. They phoned me from the hospital and told me I should go right away if I wanted to see him – they didn't think he would live. I went, but he was dead when I got there.

– Danielle died in bed. They said it was a "silent" heart attack. She said she'd just take a little nap after lunch.

– They said Jason was drunk and fell out of the hotel window. He's dead but I don't really know what happened.

– Florence had had skin cancer off and on for years. We always thought she would get well.

– We weren't surprised when Donna died. All of us in the family tried to stop her from drinking so much but she drank when we weren't around and she had bottles hidden all over the place. We knew it would happen. She forgot how many sleeping pills she had taken and died from an overdose and the liquor.

– Eric had such poor circulation after being a diabetic for so long. He was eighty. He couldn't see any more because of the bad retina, and three toes had to be amputated. He got the flu and it went to his chest and he never rallied.

– Roland took a shortcut through the lane and it was only seven o'clock, just after the store closed, and he was jumped. The doctor said he didn't feel a thing – he died instantly. The knife went right through his heart.

– There were three who were shot, but my Joan was the only one killed. Some kid did it – he was using people for target practice.

– When your husband is in the forces, you know it's possible that someday he might get killed, but you hope not.

– Clara died in her sleep. She'd had a heart condition for a few years. She didn't have pain, but she had no energy to do things.

– There was an bomb explosion at the bus depot and George died from his injuries.

– David died of pneumonia. He'd been in the nursing home for six years because of his kidneys.

– Gloria cut her wrists in the bathtub. My sister found her. They tried to revive her but she'd been there for an hour or more and we don't know why she did it. There was no note and she was not the kind of person to do that.

– Susan had a cold for a few days, then a terrible headache and high fever. We took her to the hospital. She was put in isolation and they did tests. She went worse and died.

– She was strangled. We were attacked by three men on the way to the hotel. Marjorie was small and I guess my being big and fairly strong saved me, though I was in hospital for five weeks with the injuries.

– He'd had allergies all his life. We had oxygen at home in case he needed it, but this time nothing seemed to help. Colin died as we got to the hospital.

– Wendy had been diagnosed as having non-functioning kidneys two years ago and went on dialysis regularly. I still think that she might be alive now if she could have accepted her condition, but she was always depressed.

- Lately he'd been having a little indigestion after lunch - not right away, near teatime. However, this was the worst. He was moaning and sweating. Melvin died in the ambulance.

- Everything was fine until Helen began having pains and went into labor. We were hoping for a girl. She was right on time and she'd had no trouble having our son two years ago. She died.

- After the operation Saul was never the same. He spent most of his time in the bathroom and the rest talking about what he couldn't eat. He got thinner and thinner, back and forth to the doctor and in and out of the hospital. Finally we got him into a nursing home, but he just got worse and died.

- For years, breathing was difficult for her. Glenna was allergic to almost everything, including good news. They couldn't tell us what she actually died of, but that she was not getting enough air and the lungs collapsed.

- Stephen took his own life. He shot himself in the head.

- Ross was able to get out of any door no matter what kind of lock we used and yet didn't seem to understand a thing we said. That night he got restless earlier than usual and we were all sleeping. The police found him. The doctor said he died of exposure because it was cold outside.

- Rosemarie said she was sick and tired of getting her teeth fixed and decided to have them all out and get dentures. She died from the anaesthetic or went into shock or something – she didn't wake up.

- Amanda was very ill and they said there was a chance that if she had the operation, she might improve. In the intensive care unit she developed a very high fever and then her heart stopped and they couldn't bring her around.

- Peter had Alzheimer's – he died only two years after they discovered he had it.

Appendix C
Adjustment Vignettes

Money

- "Most people I knew didn't understand why I'd be lying awake worrying because I had more money than I'd ever had after Joe died. They would say I should be so lucky, and things like that.

"I kept seeing courses advertised for women who wanted to learn more about handling money and investing so I decided to take one. It was a good idea because I found out it wasn't that hard to understand and knowing one's options makes it easier to make decisions."

- "I had no money when Jim died. Our bank account was empty. I had three children to support and didn't even know how I was going to bury Jim.

"My neighbor was a big help. She had been on social assistance and told me where to go to get help. I hated to ask, but, my children come first and I got enough money to tide me over until Jim's pension and the widow's pension benefits started."

Emotional upset

- "I was scared at night after Allan died. I had never been alone at night, even before I was married. It helped a lot when I got a cousin to come for a while. Later on, a university student rented the spare room, and I hope by spring to stay by myself."

- "It's a year now since Lydia died and I can say I'm getting along better. I couldn't have managed without help. I was very much alone. We don't have children, you see, and no relatives living here. You know, at 72, I couldn't cook at all! Lydia didn't want me in 'her' kitchen – that was her job.

"A month after she died, my doctor referred me for grief counselling and that helped some. The people in our apartment block gave me food and helped out with the laundry. Then I got a homemaker to come a couple of times a week but that's expensive, and so I went to cooking classes at the community centre. Now I do my own meals."

• "One thing I knew after Robert died was that I wanted to marry again someday. I just like being married better than being single. I stayed active socially, gave parties and was invited out often. It took me five years, but I finally met a man I really liked when I was curling in the bonspiel. We got married six months later. We love each other and love to curl."

• "It wasn't all bad when Andrew was sick. We got closer and he seemed easier to talk with – something he never could do before. He made me face his death and told me all about money and stuff. And I'm managing fine now, though I miss him, of course."

• "Charles died two months ago, and just last week when I thought nothing else bad could happen, my car was stolen. I was so mad. I was able to licence my son's old clunker and fix it up enough to use. I thought I'd forgotten how, but I found I can still drive a standard car with no trouble. If the police don't find my car I'll buy another, but meanwhile I have transportation."

Back to school

• "My husband was at home nearly all the time while he was sick. He had cancer. I had some help, thank goodness. The doctor arranged for a night nurse towards the end. I feel like I was fortunate in a way because we could both talk about his dying and now, I feel like I need to do something. It's nine months since he died and I am going to school and taking a brush-up course in typing and English. I still have a long life ahead of me (I'm 45) before retirement and I need to get a job."

In business

• "My wife and I were in business together. We both worked at our corner store. I realize now we were never apart at work and at home, it was always just the two of us. Now I am doing what we never did – I'm still working at the store, but my sons are encouraging me to make new friends. So I go to the community centre and swim and play cards after work."

The new home

• "We had moved out to the country when we retired and our home was all fixed up so beautifully. He was so good with his hands, and then he died. The trouble was, I didn't really want to be out in the sticks. I was used to the city. I was in a real bind because I couldn't sell the house, at least not for a while – the market was bad. So I gradually got involved in the local community centre and eventually became a volunteer. It's a great help to have so many new acquaintances and I'm feeling less lonely and isolated. I will probably move back to the city sometime in the next year (if I can get a good price for the house) but who knows – I may not want to sell after all."

Appendix D
Being Prepared*

Before you get seriously ill or die, consider the following suggestions. We think they would help your family and friends in a crisis.

Your relatives and business associates need to know *whom to call* and *where to find things*. The order in which we've listed our recommendations is not important. What is important is that your next of kin knows where to locate names, phone numbers and important papers if there is an emergency.

Family finances and estate planning

Your spouse or next of kin should know your outstanding debts and when accounts are due etc., power of attorney (consider it).

Will

Every adult should have a will. It's true that your spouse or next of kin will eventually get your money and property, but the key word here is *eventually*. Dying intestate (without a will) generally means it takes longer to settle an estate – a lot longer.

Money

Arrange for sufficient liquid funds, readily available for several months, for your spouse or next of kin. And each spouse should have an emergency fund in his or her own name, especially if the spouse does not have his or her own income and the bank accounts are held jointly or in your name only.

Funeral

It helps survivors if they have some idea of your burial or funeral preferences. A letter is sufficient – it doesn't have to be a legal paper. Keep a copy of this letter at home, *separate* from your will, since the will may not be read until after the burial.

Points to consider are: type of service, location of service, cemetery, cremation (ashes scattered or buried), flowers and/or donations to a charity, and cost of casket and the arrangements.

To my spouse and family:

• Some names and addresses – ask the professionals for their fee schedule so you won't be surprised when a bill arrives.

Advisors and Consultants

Financial
• for banking _____
• for accounting and tax matters _____
• for my life insurance _____

My business/work _____

Real estate _____

Other investments (e.g. pension plans, stocks) _____

Legal _____

Residence maintenance people _____

Friends _____

Others who might help you _____

Documents

A *list of important papers* is located at/in _____, or see the following for a few specific documents (such as insurance policies, burial plans, will, deeds to property, bond certificants and stock shares, bank or trust company names and addresses.)

• My *life insurance* policy is located at/in _____

• My *other insurance policies* (such as property, fire, liability etc.) are located at/in _____ (don't let premiums lapse)

• My *burial preferences* and cemetery plot arrangements are located at/in _____

• My *bank accounts* are with the following banks (include their addresses) _____

• My *will* is located at/in/with _____

• My *safety deposit box key* location is known by

_____

- My _____ is located at/in/with/_____
- My _____ is located at/in/with _____
- My _____ is located at/in/with _____

For permission to make copies, write to L.I.F.E. Resource Centre Society, #101, 395 W. Broadway, Vancouver, B.C. V5Y 1A7

Appendix E
*Information for Those Helping the Widowed**

To grieve is natural. All of us have suffered disappointments, endured losses and experienced grief in varying degrees of intensity. The death of a spouse is an overwhelming loss. It takes time and effort to adjust successfully. We can be more effective when helping the widowed if we are familiar with the grieving process and have dealt with our own feelings about death.

Responses which are not helpful to the widowed:

- Suggesting that the griever is an attractive person and will soon remarry.
- Suggesting that the widowed person has grieved long enough and should "pull up his socks and get on with his own life."
- Being uncomfortable when the bereaved person cries.
- Being unwilling to let the griever talk about the dead spouse.
- Suggesting that the widowed person is doing "so well" by displaying no visible signs of grief.
- Excluding the griever from social activities because he or she is no longer part of a couple.

Responses which are helpful to the widowed:

Acknowledging the death with a simple statement of sympathy such as:

- I'm very sorry to hear of your loss.
- I am very sorry to hear of _____'s death.
- I'm so sorry _____ died.
- Please accept my sympathy.
- I don't know what to say except I'm sorry and I think about you.

During the shock, numbness and disbelief period, give practical assistance:

- Help make funeral arrangements.
- Cook food, water plants, clean up, empty garbage, feed the pets, and so on.
- Check on whether help is available on practical matters, such as probating the will or applying for Canada Pension benefits and other financial assistance.

During the realization of loss period:

- Allow the widowed person to talk about the dead spouse.
- Talk about the deceased as having died even though the griever may use euphemisms (passed away, passed on, gone).
- Discuss some of the feelings that grieving people usually have.
- Encourage moderate exercise such as walking.
- Encourage expression of emotions. Crying relieves tension and feelings need to be expressed.
- Encourage the bereaved person to pay attention to eating habits. Widowed people often lose their appetites and forget about meals.
- Ask if there had been periods of depression when the spouse was alive. If so, adjustment may take longer.
- Sleeping patterns may change. Suggest writing in a journal, doing relaxation exercises or reading something comforting.
- Encourage routine activities that help give structure to daily living.
- Help the widowed person find advice on legal matters, and suggest they update their own will.

During the letting go and acceptance period:

- If the personal effects of the spouse have not been disposed of, offer to help with this.
- Encourage the bereaved person to become involved in something new or to resume formerly enjoyable activities.
- Discuss what direction the widowed person sees his or her life taking and what options are available.

Factors that help the griever to successful adjustment

- A positive attitude towards life.
- A feeling of self worth.
- Being self-reliant and independent.
- Having emotional and practical support from other people.
- Having a job or interest that provides continuity.
- Ability to talk about feelings.

Factors that tend to prolong the grief process

- Medical history of depression.
- Life-long pessimistic attitude.
- Chronic health problems.
- Lack of self-esteem.
- The widowed person may have few friends because of a life pattern of doing everything with his or her spouse or because of lengthy illness of the spouse.
- Fear of being physically alone.
- Dependence on the spouse (the widowed person has no experience in managing finances and making independent decisions.)
- Reluctance to let go of the past.
- No ongoing interests.
- Several losses occurring close together, e.g. death of another close person, divorce in the family, loss of job.
- Difficulty in talking about feelings.
- Unnatural deaths, e.g. murder, accident, missing person, suicide.
- Has not adjusted to a previous loss, e.g. death of a parent five years ago.

* © *Revised 1985 Elsie Palmer & Jill Watt.*

For information write to the L.I.F.E. Resource Centre, #101, 395 West Broadway, Vancouver, B.C., V5Y 1A7

Appendix F
Phone Numbers of People and Services

The following is a list of services and people to remind you of phone numbers that friends and employees may need when they offer help during the first few weeks after the death of your spouse:

Accountant, air conditioning, airlines, associations, antiques, artists, automobile, babysitters, bank, bakery, barber, Better Business Bureau, bookstore, bus information, car, carpenter, caterer, chimney sweep, church, city hall, cleaners, clothing stores, clubs, computer, cottage, craft specialists, credit cards, dentist, department stores, doctors, druggist, electric company, electrician, fabric store, fish market, florist, furnace repair, funeral director, gardener, gas company, government services, hairdresser, hardware, health spa, heating oil, hospitals, insurance (property, health, life), investment counsellor, jeweller, kennels, landlord, landscaping, laundry, lawyer, library, lumberyard, magazines, marina, movers, municipal hall, museums, newspaper, notary, nursery school, nurseries, nursing home, office supplies, optician, optometrist, orthodontist, painter, pharmacy, photographer, plumber, post office, public health department, radio, real estate, restaurants, roof and eaves, refuse removal, schools, septic tank service, service station, ski conditions, snow removal, social security, sporting goods, stationery store, stock broker, supermarket, tailor, taxi, telephone company, telegraph office, television repair, towing service, train information, travel agent, tree service, typewriter, upholsterers, utility company, veterinarian, video store, voter information, watch repair, weather forecast, window cleaner, yard work, yarn shop.

Appendix G
How to Start a Bereavement Support Group

For the purposes of a newly bereaved self-help group, *newly bereaved* may be defined as someone whose spouse has died within the past year or year and a half, and who feels she or he is not adjusting.

Who might want to start a support group?

People who have been widowed and feel that they would have benefited had they had a support group when they were grieving. It is usually someone who has adjusted and who wants to use that experience to help others.

A professional person who, when visiting widowed people, may see that the patients or clients could benefit from getting together with others who are widowed.

What does support mean in this context?

It means emotional and social support – people who care about you, call and visit you and offer help, people who like and love you, who make you feel like you are still part of the family and the community.

What would the widowed get out of a support group?

There are several reasons why a widowed person might come to a support group.

- She or he may now, since the death of the husband or wife, be the last person in their family.
- Geographical distance may separate him or her from family members; the couple may have retired far from family and friends. Or the widowed person may have recently come from another country, state of province and may not have relatives and friends nearby.
- Personality may affect adjustment. The widowed person may

not have friends and family to talk with if their manner is unusual or offensive.

- If the spouse was ill for a long time and the couple were no longer socially active, the widowed person may have very few friends, if any, when the spouse dies.
- Some widowed people find that their friends, family and relatives don't understand what they are feeling and what they are going through. They think that if they could get together with people who understand and share their emotions, they wouldn't feel so alone.

Types of support groups

There are two main types of support groups – continuous entry and cyclical.

A cyclical support group is a course of six to ten sessions, held once a week, with ten to fifteen participants. A continuous entry group, on the other hand, is ongoing all year. It takes people in whenever they ask to come, and they can stay as long as they find it helpful.

The advantage of the continuous entry group is that the bereaved person doesn't have to wait until the next program or course begins. If he phones on a Monday and the group meets on Fridays, he has only a few days to wait. If the group meets twice a month, the longest waiting time would be two weeks.

The disadvantage to the continuous entry group is that widowed people may want to continue in the group after they have adjusted because they have formed friendships and feel comfortable there.

Talking to potential members

Most people attending a bereavement group have never been in a self-help group before. Therefore, the person who talks to them about the bereavement support group should explain what goes on in the meeting or session. For instance, tell them that they would have an opportunity to talk about how they are feeling, about their situation, about personal things that are happening to them. However, the interviewer or facilitator should also assure the widowed person that they will not be expected to enter into the discussion *unless they want to.*

At this time, the facilitator can determine whether the client needs to be referred to another service that might be more appropriate, or whether he or she may benefit from private counselling.

It is easier for the griever if the person who interviews them is the facilitator of the group, so that the participant coming into the group knows at least one member.

At the meeting

In a bereavement group, new widows and/or widowers talk about themselves and what is happening to them *among themselves,* and the facilitator's job is to make sure everyone has an opportunity to speak. The facilitator provides information about the grief process and observes the individuals' reactions to what is being said, so as to be able to address the special concerns of each group member.

The facilitator must be someone who has experienced a traumatic grief in his or her own life and who has fully adjusted to the loss. Education in grief counselling is also essential. He or she should be capable and willing to lead the group, whether employed by the group or as a volunteer.

The group facilitator will encourage participants to:

- participate: express feelings and responsively listen to others.
- be non-judgmental: accept each person's viewpoint as being valid and worth consideration.
- show compassion: be concerned about both themselves and others.
- appreciate uniqueness: no one can fill another's place in the group. Each person's ideas and opinions are important.
- have fun: laughter and humor are as necessary as tears.

The support group should emphasize the need for a friendly atmosphere at the meetings – one which protects the participants' confidentiality as much as possible, encourages non-judgmental discussion, and demonstrates caring, willingness to listen, and willingness to share feelings and thoughts.

Evaluation

It is important to occasionally evaluate the progress participants are making towards adjustment.

A questionnaire can be typed and distributed for clients to fill in and return anonymously. Some useful questions are:

- How long have you been in the bereavement group?
- What benefits do you get from the group meeting?

      1 _____
      2 _____
      3 _____

- What is the *most important* thing *for you* about the group meeting?
- How much longer do you think you will need the group meeting?
- What else would you like to see happen in the group meeting?
- What do you like *least* about the group meeting?

When the bereavement group is part of a large organization

A bereavement group that is part of a large organization – such as a church, community centre or social service agency – has several advantages over a separate one. First, the organizers probably know the widowed people who could benefit and it would be easy to notify them of the new program being offered; the bereavement support group would be offered along with the other services the organization provides.

The start-up time for this group would probably not be as long as with a separate association or group, and a framework for financing the group may already be in place within the larger organization. There may well be funds available immediately for the group.

In addition, the grievers would be in a familiar place. They already know people there and they feel comfortable. The facilitator might be someone they have already met – the director of programs, for example – and that could be a big advantage.

L.I.F.E. (Living Is For Everyone) Resource Centre

In 1972 in Vancouver, there was no organization addressing the special needs of widows. The L.I.F.E. program was designed to fill this gap by offering widows emotional support, practical information and referrals during the difficult adjustment to single status.

The L.I.F.E. Resource Centre, founded by Elsie Palmer, started with one self-help support group meeting once a week, and one social group meeting on the first Sunday of each month. The YWCA provided the meeting room. The first meeting was a discussion on the need for a group, how to finance it, and how to reach widows needing information and emotional support.

Starting a support group for bereaved people

Someone has the idea to start a self-help organization, and she or he calls a meeting of everyone who may be interested in such a group.

After establishing the need for a bereavement support group, committees of two or three people each are formed to look into the following considerations and to bring back their findings and recommendations to the next organizers' meeting.

Funding

Is money needed for room rental, salaries, advertising, brochures, office equipment or supplies? Where to get it? Grants, donations, a benefactor, memberships, user fees?

Number of clients

How many widowed people are you expecting to be interested in a support group? Should it be limited?

The number of participants at meetings doesn't matter too much. A minimum of five and maximum of nine works well for discussions and self-disclosure sessions. If there are more than nine people at the meeting, the facilitator should divide them into several small groups and then bring them together again after fifteen minutes or so.

Will the bereavement support group be for widowed people and/or will there be separate sessions for men and women?

Meetings and meeting place

Establish the time, place, and frequency of regular meetings.

The meeting place will depend on the number of people anticipated for the group sessions, and on whether proximity to public transportation and parking lots are factors to consider.

If many clients will depend on public transportation, a meeting time during the day is usually preferable.

Individual counselling

Develop a policy for referring clients for private counselling. Is the group facilitator qualified to counsel as well?

Advertising and publicity

Outlets to be considered for advertising the new support group include the following: local papers, radio, TV, church bulletins, laundromats, and library notice boards. Notify other groups, such as the city health and social services department, insurance companies and funeral homes.

Guidelines for participants
in the bereavement self-help group

Goal: To adjust to a new situation – being single.

Objectives:

- initiate an activity with another person once a week
- become involved in an ongoing group activity (besides the bereavement support group)
- have physical health assessed and make a decision to improve it
- be able to state and feel responsible for at least one thing to like and appreciate about herself or himself
- experience pleasure and good feelings
- build self-confidence and be aware of options and choices

Appendix H
Suggested Reading

Before buying one of the books in our selected reading list, visit or telephone your nearest library and ask if they have it. If not, telephone a bookstore and ask whether they stock the book. If they don't, ask how much the book is, whether there is a paperback edition, and how long it would take if they ordered it for you. Another bookstore may have what you want, so call a few bookstores before placing a special order, as you may have to wait as long as six weeks.

For widowers

Kohn, Jane Burgess and Willard K. Kohn. *The Widower: What He Faces, What He Feels, What He Needs.* Beacon, 1978.

Lewis, C.S. *A Grief Observed.* Seabury Press, 1963.

Weakman, Sidney. *Only a Little Time: Memoir of My Wife.* Little, Brown & Co., 1972.

For widows

Loewinsohn, Ruth J. *Survival Handbook for Widows.* Scott, Foresman and Co. and AARP, revised edition 1984.

Peterson, James A. and Michael Briley. *Widows & Widowhood: A Creative Approach to Being Alone.* Association Press, 1977.

Taves, Isabella. *The Widow's Guide.* Schocken Books, 1981.

Wylie, Betty Jane. *Beginnings: A Book for Widows.* McClelland and Stewart, 1977.

Personal experiences of grief

Caine, Lynn. *Widow.* William Morrow, 1974.

Grollman, Earl A. *What Helped Me when my Loved One Died.* Beacon, 1981.

Hersey, Jean. *A Widow's Pilgrimage*. Seabury, 1979.

Hsu, Dorothy. *Mending: The Pain and Healing of a Widow's First Year*. David C. Cook, 1979.

Phipps, J. *Death's Single Privacy: Grieving and Personal Growth*. Seabury Press, 1974.

Stearns, Ann Kaiser. *Living through Personal Crisis*. Thomas More Press, 1984.

Children and grief

Grollman, Earl A. *Talking about Death: Dialogue between Parent and Child*. Beacon Press, 1977.

Knowles, Donald W. and Nancy Reeves. *But Won't Granny Need Her Socks? Dealing Effectively with Children's Concerns about Death and Dying*. Kendall Hunt, 1983.

Krementz, Jill. *How It Feels when a Parent Dies*. Alfred A. Knopf, 1981.

LeShan, Eda. *Learning to Say Goodbye: When a Parent Dies*. Macmillan, 1976.

Sharapan, Hedda Bluestone. *Talking with Young Children about Death*. Family Communications, 1979.

Other books on bereavement

Colgrove, Melba, H. Bloomfield and P. McWilliams. *How to Survive the Loss of a Love*. Leo Press, 1976.

Danto, Bruce and Austin Kutscher. *Suicide and Bereavement*. Arno Press, 1977.

Davidson, Glen. W. *Understanding Mourning: A Guide for Those who Grieve*. Religion and Medicine Series of Augsburg Publishing House, 1984.

Hewett, John. *After Suicide*. Westminster Press, 1980.

Knapp, Ronald J. *Beyond Endurance: When a Child Dies*. Schocken Books, 1986.

Kushner, Harold S. *When Bad Things Happen to Good People*. Schocken Books, 1981.

O'Connor, Nancy. *Letting Go with Love: The Grieving Process*. La Mariposa Press, 1984.

Schiff, Harriet S. *The Bereaved Parent*. Penguin, 1978.

Schneiderman, Gerald. *Coping with Death in the Family*. NC Press, revised edition 1985.

Tatebaum, Judy. *The Courage to Grieve*. Lipincott & Crowell, 1980.

Self-help

Allen, Jeffery G. *How to Turn an Interview into a Job*. Simon & Schuster, 1983.

Bloomfield, Harold H. *Making Peace with Your Parents*. Ballantine Books, 1983.

Bolles, Richard N. *The Three Boxes of Life and How to Get Out of Them: An Introduction to Life Planning*. Ten Speed Press, 1978.

Costello, Brian. *Your Money and How to Keep It*. Stoddart, revised edition 1985.

Donoghue, William. *Lifetime Financial Planner*. Harper & Row, 1987.

Dyer, Wayne W. *Pulling Your Own Strings*. Funk & Wagnall, 1978.

Friedman, Sonya. *Smart Cookies Don't Crumble: A modern woman's guide to living and loving her own life*. G.P. Putnam's Sons, 1985

Kassorla, Irene C. *Go for It! How to Win at Love, Work and Play*. Dell Publishing, 1984.

Philips, Gerald M. *Help for shy people and anyone else who ever felt ill at ease on entering a room full of strangers*. Prentice-Hall, 1981.

Wylie, Betty Jane and Lynne MacFarlane. *Every Woman's Money Book*. Key Porter Books, 1984.

For professionals and those helping the bereaved

Morgan, Ernest. *Dealing Creatively with Death: A Manual of Death Education and Simple Burial*. Celo Press, 1984.

Rando, Therese A. *Grief, Dying and Death: Clinical Interventions for Caregivers*. Research Press Company, 1984.

Worden, J. William. *Grief Counseling and Grief Therapy*. Springer, 1982.